Make Every Word Count:

A Structured Approach to Build and Deliver High Impact Analytic Products

By Jay Grusin, PhD and Steve Lindo

Intelligent Risk Management Publications

Endorsements

"Make Every Word Count" is a unique instructional manual for intelligence analysis, as it combines the knowledge and expertise of Jay Grusin, a 29-year veteran of the U.S. government's analytic trenches, and Steve Lindo, a deeply experienced international business risk manager. Both authors demonstrate the universal applicability of *Intelligence Analysis* methodology for improving decision-making. The book's emphasis on methodical structure will help inexperienced analysts develop not only the correct process, but also the right mindset, to succeed in their profession."

—Michael Ard
Program Director, MS in Intelligence Analysis,
Johns Hopkins Advanced Academic Programs,
Johns Hopkins University, Washington D.C

"This book is a must-read for analysts working in government and in any industry who strive to write succinct, value-added assessments for senior audiences. Analytic writing is a craft that must be learned, and this book provides an excellent, systematic process to teach analysts how to do the critical thinking up front, which ultimately leads to much more sophisticated analytic products. I have used many of these techniques to train CIA analysts, as well as hundreds of students at the Naval Postgraduate School, and fully endorse the authors' approaches."

—John D. Tullius
Faculty Lecturer
Naval Postgraduate School, Monterey
Former National Intelligence Chair

"Dr. Grusin and Steve Lindo offer analysts of all stripes a highly compelling, accessible approach to analysis based on decades of experience in the US intelligence community."

—Matt Berrett
Director of Analytics, Space Dynamics Lab
Cofounder, The Center for Anticipatory Intelligence, Utah State University

Endorsements

"This book promises to be a much-needed primer for those who wish to think and communicate efficiently and effectively in any number of fields. Building upon decades of experience in the intelligence community and business consulting, Grusin and Lindo lead the reader through a logical pathway from starting to think about an issue to how to frame a logical and easily understood explanation of the things that matter related to the issue. This book should be required reading for anyone seeking ways to understand the complexity around them more effectively."

—**Karl Kaltenthaler, PhD**
Director of the Michael J. Morell Center for Intelligence and Security Studies
Professor, Department of Political Science,The University of Akron

"I was fortunate to have worked with Jay after he retired from the CIA. He brought his expertise and techniques for intelligence analysis to the corporate world. Jay and Steve's approach to developing actionable intelligence is directly applicable to the process of analyzing client needs and building valuable complex solutions for both private and public sectors."

—**Jim Allen**
Principal
Response Resource, Washinton D.C.

"I wish I had had Grusin and Lindo's books earlier in my career. They provide a valuable framework for creating actionable analysis and teach us techniques honed over decades in the intelligence community and translated to the business world. The latest book goes a step further than the first and guides the reader step-by-step through the process—becoming a desktop reference book that you will use time and again."

—**Tim Hicks**
Principal TCH Consulting
Former Chief Operations Officer, Heidrick & Struggles

Make Every Word Count:
A Structured Approach to Build and Deliver
High Impact Analytic Products

By Jay Grusin, PhD, and Stephen Lindo

First Edition September 2024

ISBN: 978-1-7373019-2-9

Published in the United States by
Intelligent Risk Management Publications
6224 Cowell Road
Brighton, Michigan 48116
www.IntelligentRiskManagement.solutions

Book Design, Cover and Typesetting by
Cynthia J. Kwitchoff (CJKCREATIVE.COM)

Note to Readers: Disclaimer

ABOUT THE AUTHORS

Dr. Jay Grusin has served as an intelligence analyst and manager and teacher of analysts for over 40 years.

In 2008, he completed a 29-plus-year career at the Central Intelligence Agency, and since then has provided management and intelligence training across the private and public sectors. He also serves on the Advisory Board of the Michael J. Morell Center for Intelligence and Security Studies at the University of Akron.

Dr. Grusin is a member of the CIA's Senior Intelligence Service and received the Agency's Distinguished Career Intelligence Medal in recognition of his contributions, which include helping create and deliver an analytic training course that redefined how intelligence analysis would be taught at the CIA and led the development/delivery of the first sequenced management/ leadership curriculum.

Beginning in 2018, Dr. Grusin teamed with Steve Lindo to establish Intelligent Risk Management LLC. Together they developed and delivered a series of workshops, and now this book, for private sector clients based on how to apply these same tools and processes to help identify and manage risk and uncertainty.

Dr. Grusin earned his MA and PhD at the University of Arizona. He and his wife, Sarah, live outside of Ann Arbor, MI.

Steve Lindo is a financial risk manager with over 30 years' experience managing risks in banking, asset management and insurance.

He is Co-Principal of Intelligent Risk Management LLC, an executive education and advisory partnership which uses analytical methods pioneered by the US intelligence services to enhance decision-making by enterprises across all industries. Since 2014 he has been a part-time lecturer in Columbia University's Master of Science in Enterprise Risk Management program.

Mr. Lindo's earlier career includes executive positions with Fifth Third Bancorp, GMAC Financial Services (now Ally Financial), Cargill Financial Services, First National Bank of Chicago (now part of JPMorgan Chase) and Lloyds Bank, in the US, UK, Spain and Brazil.

In 2010, Mr. Lindo completed a two-year engagement as Executive Director of PRMIA – The Professional Risk Managers' International Association, a non-profit member organization with over 75,000 members in 198 countries.

Mr. Lindo is a regular presenter at conferences, webinar host and author of risk management articles and case studies.

He has a BA and MA from Oxford University and speaks fluent French, German, Spanish and Portuguese. He and his wife Marcie live near their grandchildren in Columbus, Ohio.

BY THE SAME AUTHORS

"Intelligent Analysis: How to Defeat Uncertainty in High-Stakes Decisions"

Published by: Intelligent Risk Management Publications, June 2021.
Available in print and Kindle form.
SBN: 978-1-7373019-0-5

Making good decisions involving high stakes and uncertainty requires a significantly different mindset from an organization's default decision-making process, which is typically dictated by culture, hierarchy, personalities, data, and haste. The methods described in this book, honed over decades by the US Intelligence Services, emphasize discipline, objectivity, diversity, reason, and transparency. Most importantly, they don't interfere with the way your organization makes its high-stakes decisions. Instead, they add a protective layer of analytics that either validates a good decision, or exposes the flaws which could lead to catastrophic consequences. Regardless of your organization's risk tolerance, these methods will show you where a high-stakes decision you have to make lies on the uncertainty spectrum and what, if any, actions you can take to nudge the needle to the left.

TABLE OF CONTENTS

ACKNOWLEDGMENTS

Our last book served two audiences: senior executives "and the analysts that support them." Writing for two audiences was challenging. Given Jay's background, he suggested a second book aimed solely at reaching a wider swath of analysts, both practicing and aspiring. Equally important, we wanted to reach readers who may not see themselves ("who me?") as analysts, but in fact are doing that work every day—collecting and analyzing data and drawing inferences about what's next—and should see themselves as one of us.

With this goal in mind, we approached a range of outside readers from different backgrounds to comment and offer suggestions to strengthen our message. We asked them to answer two critical questions to see if we were on track: would it serve as a guide for developing analytic products; and would it serve as a textbook? Their comments and insights are woven into the fabric of the text and serve as their contribution to our goal of "building" analysts.

The response was yes to both questions, often followed by "but what about…" Their invaluable suggestions and insights impacted every facet of the book and repeatedly sent us back to revise our many drafts. Most important, their comments prompted us to rethink how to further clarify some key concepts since our last book was published three years ago.

In terms of reviewing, my first stop is always my wife, Sarah, a terrific writer in her own right, who reviewed the first draft and as always posed multiple provocative questions that helped us sharpen our message. She also pushed hard for changing the original title, which none of the readers liked, that now aligns more closely with our message.

Our other reviewers each made substantive contributions. From the commercial world my co-author, Steve, of course, always brings his forty years of risk management experience, a unique perspective and a strong sense of how to reach a wide audience. We also drew heavily on Tim Hicks, a management consultant with decades of experience. Tim was not shy (really not shy) about pointing out the lack of clarity at key junctures and made suggestions that would help the content resonate with managers of analysts in the commercial world. Dan Luria, a senior economist focused on development, reinforced the message on use of unfamiliar terms. He also brought his expertise to bear on technical issues, especially on making the application scenario more realistic throughout the book.

We continued to draw on my former colleagues from the Central Intelligence Agency (CIA), all of whom have been engaged in different settings since retiring. While they all said yes to our two critical questions, they saw other areas that needed attention. My close friend and colleague Marty Petersen, a former senior CIA officer and tradecraft expert, pointed out multiple points for further clarification and suggested making the role of consumers more central to our process. For his part, Frans Bax did much the same but added important insights on the need to provide more specific support for instructors who might adopt the book for course work. As a result, we decided to craft an Instructor Guide and offer online support as needed.

Two other readers occupy academic positions that focus on intelligence analysis. Dale Avery, an instructor at Embry-Riddle Aeronautical University, shared his teaching materials and suggested that I add emphasis on writing, which is reflected in additional emphasis at key points and in the last chapter that further reinforce the importance of careful drafting and self-reviewing. I also wish to acknowledge Matt Berrett, Director of Analytics, Space Dynamics Lab, and Cofounder of Utah State University's Center for Anticipatory Intelligence. Matt appreciated our effort to reach a broader audience of analysts. Equally important, at his suggestion we added a section that emphasizes the importance of using self-assessment instruments to help analysts become more aware of unconscious biases that can impact objectivity.

On the production side…

Edited by: Art Milch of ProofreadingPal, LLC.

and

Book Design, Cover and Typesetting by: Cynthia Kwitchoff of CJKCreative.com who again made our book shine.

Jay Grusin: JRGrusin@gmail.com
Steve Lindo: Steve.Lindo@gmail.com

PREFACE BY JAY GRUSIN

"Thinking analytically is a skill like carpentry or driving a car. It can be taught, it can be learned, and it can improve with practice."

—Richards J. Heuer,
Psychology of Intelligence Analysis

Every word does count.

I learned this lesson early in my thirty-year career as an analyst at the CIA. After working all day on my first analytic product for senior US government officials, my reviewer stood next to me and said (firmly) something like: "I am not clear about what you are trying to say here, and I am not sure how it would be helpful." My consumer needed actionable intelligence—analysis that consumers could act on—and my first piece unsurprisingly failed. I finally got it right at around ten o'clock that evening. For added emphasis, on my first day my manager said (again, firmly) that my job every day is to meet consumers' requirements with targeted analysis that answers their questions with objective, forward-looking analysis that is clearly written and delivered on time. And as I learned every day, that is no easy task.

I came to the job equipped with deep substantive expertise and understanding of the "why" of the CIA's mission, but not of the "how"—the hard mechanics—of meeting those requirements. Over time, I became increasingly proficient in speed, accuracy, and quality, and to my good fortune I eventually became a highly successful intelligence trainer working with hundreds of analysts and their managers. And even after over forty-two years as an analyst my passion for the work remains undiminished.

The skills I gained came with repetition, feedback, and a commitment to learn the "how." And you can do the same if the will and patience are there. As analysts, regardless of where we work or what we do, we want our work to matter, to have an impact, to add value for our consumers. We want to help them identify and manage risk and uncertainty and reach their goals while increasing their awareness of risk and opportunities that can impact their organizations.

Our structured approach—*Intelligent Analysis*—coaches you through a proven step-by-step path to consistently produce objective and data-driven analytic assessments. It is hands-on and heavily experiential, not theory. It combines the same tools and processes—known as analytic tradecraft, or simply tradecraft—that I relied on and taught for thirty years as a senior analyst at the CIA. Then factor in another twelve plus years as a contractor training analysts in multiple settings. My co-author, Steve Lindo, brings another four decades of experience in risk management to the book. In addition, my experience baked a set of core values into my analytic DNA that are embedded in our process. They are inseparable from the work.

Intelligent Analysis has proven effective well beyond the US intelligence services. It has been taught in business schools. It has also proven effective in boosting the skills of practicing and aspiring analysts with roles in the private sector, government contracting, law enforcement agencies, and the legal profession. It has been applied as well in academic settings and professional schools.

Make Every Word Count is formatted as a combined text and complementary Workbook. It is heavily practice-based and, building on your own work or project, moves you through each chapter. Our approach is tightly structured and formatted. It is unique in that, rather than focus on developing lengthy analyses, it focuses on building the lead paragraph, the Bottom Line Up Front (B.L.U.F.) *before you draft*. This paragraph's format is fixed in concrete, and the sentences are sequenced to send a consistently clear message to consumers. Structured Analytic Techniques (SATs), explained first in the Key Terms below, then in-depth in Chapter 1 and at each step in our process, provide templates that illustrate "how to" with an example of each step and then show you how to apply it to your own work. When completed they become the basis for drafting analytic products of any length.

The Workbook, a downloadable MS Word document which is available by sending an email request to **MakeEveryWordCount.2024@gmail.com**, will coach you through the process and can be used for your own future products. Over time, if you do the work, *Intelligent Analysis* will become second nature.

> **Note:** In the Workbook the exercises for each chapter are listed in the Table of Contents. The exercises are in the same order in each Workbook chapter and also numbered to make it easier to track your progress.

For analysts, both practicing and aspiring, we offer four big takeaways:

- **First, see yourself in the work.** Regardless of where you work or what you do, you are an analyst if you collect and analyze data and assess its significance by telling consumers in a written or oral presentation what story it tells. By using your own work and working through the chapters you can start to see the possibilities that come with being conscious and deliberate about how you approach analytic work.

- **Second, embrace the analysts' core values.** Again we emphasize that keeping an intense focus on the consumer and maintaining objectivity are non-negotiable and inseparable from the process.

- **Third, gain self-assurance.** Your confidence as an analyst will grow as tradecraft skills and the underlying core values seep into your mental DNA. You will find yourself more confident in your ability to craft, explain, and defend your analysis regardless of your consumer's rank or position.

- **Fourth, join our community.** My daughter Claire once observed that what I do is "build analysts," and I like that turn of phrase. In *Make Every Word Count*, Steve and I see *Intelligent Analysis* as something of a construction product.

Our experience shows that if you apply the rigorous and disciplined tools and processes set out in our book, you will be a more effective and confident analyst. Think of our methodical and disciplined approach as an insurance policy, a check against the mental errors that can often occur under the time and emotional pressures that come with the daily requirements to produce objective, timely assessments for multiple consumers.

Finally, a senior officer and good friend at the CIA drew an analogy between the work of CIA analysts and their counterparts in CIA operations who were trained in "jumping out of airplanes," asserting that doing intelligence analysis can be equally challenging because the stakes can be so high.

PREFACE BY STEVE LINDO

Credit analysts, risk managers, lawyers, and product managers—these are just some of the job titles that qualify as analysts for the purposes of this book. In my case, during twenty plus years in banking, I performed hundreds of credit analyses, ranging from working capital finance for a small supplier of hardwoods in the Amazon, to co-financing the rail tunnel under the English Channel. Many credit analysts, risk managers, and product managers are, of course, justifiably proud of their analytical skills without ever having heard of *Intelligent Analysis*. However, the flow of business dictates that their skills are primarily honed by training and experience in the analysis of familiar risks. What *Intelligent Analysis* brings is a methodology specifically designed to expose and mitigate uncertainties, as well as the curses of group-think, emotions, cognitive biases, and organizational influence, which hinder analytical objectivity in unfamiliar situations.

By way of example, a credit analysis I recall vividly was for cofinancing a nuclear power plant in Spain. My team of credit analysts was tasked with creating a ten-year cash flow forecast against a backdrop of macroeconomic trends, global energy prices, controlled electricity tariffs, and unknown nuclear waste disposal costs—a complex cocktail of quantitative and qualitative data to sort through. Also, our analysis had to walk a tightrope between the Madrid-based business development team in hot pursuit of the deal and our regional credit Senior Vice President in London who carried a long-standing prejudice against nuclear power. Did we get stuck trying to make a recommendation based on a credible cash flow forecast? Yes, a number of times, but we muddled through, and the deal finally got done. In hindsight, how much better our analysis would have been if we had been able to draw on the methods described in this book.

Two innate strengths of my hand-picked Madrid credit team were patient and persistent research and uncompromising objectivity, which echo a recurring theme in this book: that analysts' mindset, conduct, and self-confidence are also fundamental to achieving the most credible analysis.

Another essential ingredient in providing impactful analysis (which we call "actionable intelligence") of business decisions is carving and carving again the recommendation supported by the analysis until its essence can be summarized in a single paragraph and then in a one-sentence inference. There were many occasions during my later years as a risk manager when my time-challenged audience needed a fifteen-second answer in order to incorporate my view on a high stakes risk situation into their decision.

I recall two specific discussions, one about cutting cross-border risks to Brazil, and one about potential losses from SUV auto leases if gas prices were to double. While completely unrelated in time and circumstance, both decisions had major revenue and profit implications for their respective business lines. In each case, knowing that a risk recommendation was needed at a specific meeting, my team of analysts had time to diligently sift through the relevant data beforehand and arrive at a recommendation. But I, in the room, had only fifteen seconds to state my case and the analysis which supported it. Distilling the team's analysis into the sound bite that would meet the audience's requirements (creating a "B.L.U.F." in our vernacular) was crucial to impacting their decision. Learning how to do so took years of trial and error. I wish I had this book to help me then.

Many day-to-day business decisions proceed successfully by using familiar analytical content, quite justifiably. The challenge met by this book occurs when analysts confront uncertain, unfamiliar, and emotionally charged situations. There is no instant fix for this, but rather the painstaking acquisition and mastery of processes designed specifically for such situations. This book will show you how.

Looking forward, the practice of analytics is currently entering uncharted waters driven by advanced computer-based analytical methods which fall under the general description of artificial intelligence (AI). While some industry forecasters may argue that the kind of slow-thinking, causal analysis characterized by *Intelligent Analysis* will become obsolete, Jay and I strongly disagree. Just as the objective assessment of a complex, high-stakes situation relies on accurately identifying the Key Intelligence Question (Chapter 3), so too decision-supporting data collated by generative AI methods rely on situation-appropriate prompts. Making sure that such prompts accurately align with the Working and Key Assumptions (Chapter 7) which underlie the situation's desired outcome is a perfect application for *Intelligent Analysis*.

Clarifying Key Terms: Read These First

To avoid any misunderstandings, we list below some of the terms used early on in the book that may differ from more widely understood definitions. A complete glossary of terms used in the book is in Appendix B. We see the following terms as essential to understanding Intelligent Analysis:

Actionable intelligence: This term describes targeted assessments that consumers (see below) can act on.

Analytic product (or simply product): In contrast to its more generally understood definition, "product" as used here to refers to an assessment drafted using *Intelligent Analysis*.

Assumption: As used in *Intelligent Analysis*, an assumption is a condition that must persist to support the estimated level of probability that the consumer will reach the desired outcome, or whether an event or development will occur; the estimated probability must be subject to change with new information. The term "variable" is often used interchangeably with "assumption" but is tied more closely to economics and math.

Bottom Line on the Bottom (B.L.O.B.): This term describes a written assessment in which the main point or message does not become apparent until the end of the piece; it is most common in academic papers and journals but banned in *Intelligent Analysis*.

Bottom Line Up Front (B.L.U.F.): This term refers to the tightly structured and formatted lead paragraph required in an analytic product that gives consumers a complete answer to their question, including an estimated probability of whether they will reach their desired end-state or a particular event or development will occur.

Caveat: For our purposes, caveats are a group of terms (*likely, unlikely, highly likely,* etc.…) used across the US intelligence services to inform or warn consumers of the strength of the relationship between the facts and what can be inferred from those facts. For example, "The event is (likely…) to take place."

Consumer: This term is generally understood to mean an individual who purchases goods for personal use. However, among the US intelligence services it generally refers to end users of intelligence products inside the US government and military. In our book we broaden that definition well beyond that narrow application to include end users of analytic products in multiple settings both inside and outside the intelligence services, including, for example, decision makers, strategic planners, legal and law enforcement professionals, business developers and contractors, researchers inside and outside academia, or students engaged in undergraduate or graduate/professional studies.

Inference: This is defined for our purposes as a conclusion based on facts as known. In this book inferences are structured as A + B → C. A and B are facts as known and C is the inference or insight/conclusion that can be drawn. The arrow (→) is a stand-in for the estimate of probability that C will occur (*likely, unlikely*, etc.), expressed using an agreed-upon vocabulary.

Intelligent Analysis: An approach to delivering analytic products across business areas that combines private sector risk-management methods with the tools and processes the US intelligence services have used for decades to support senior US government officials, especially structured analytic techniques (SATs) (see below and Chapter 1), to help filter out the emotions and biases that work against objective analysis.

Key Assumptions Check (KAC): This was developed as a framework that is part of the suite of SATs intended to test the validity of the assumptions and level of confidence in the data underpinning the inference and their potential impact on the estimate of probability of the inference.

Key Intelligence Question (KIQ): This is the question developed collaboratively between analysts and the audience that answers a specific question; it is crafted against a set of criteria and answered in the B.L.U.F.

Structured Analytic Techniques (SATs): These are widely understood as a suite of qualitative frameworks that rely on structured discussions to help analysts mitigate the adverse impact on objective analysis of their cognitive limitations—biases, emotions, and mindsets that work against objective analysis.

INTRODUCTION

The How and Why of *Make Every Word Count*

"Analysts should be self-conscious about their reasoning processes. They should think about how they make judgments and reach conclusions, not just about the judgments and conclusions themselves."

—Richards Heuer (*Psychology of Intelligence Analysis*)

We agree that analysts must be deliberate and conscious in crafting their assessments. The structure of *Intelligent Analysis* encourages you as analysts to slow down and use our process to work through what you want to say. What is your analytic message, and is the line of reasoning in it transparent to consumers, defensible, and repeatable?

And it needs to be actionable, aimed at meeting consumers' requirements that the analysis help them manage uncertainty and risk and improve the likelihood that they will achieve their goals. These demands mean that understanding and meeting consumers' changing requirements and agendas is the heart of our approach.

For practicing and aspiring analysts in any field striving every day to do their best, *Make Every Word Count* is a powerful toolkit which will position you to produce well-crafted objective and actionable analysis that will increase your impact and value added regardless of where you work or what you do. *Intelligent Analysis* will get you there. It offers analysts a carefully structured, step-by-set process that can change how they do their work and, perhaps as important, to think about themselves as analysts. With clarity and rigor, you will be better positioned to meet your organization's shifting requirements, identify risks and opportunities, look ahead to assess the most likely outcome,and implications for your consumers and mitigation strategies to manage risks.

First, we define how we use the term. *Intelligent Analysis* is an approach to delivering any analytic product that combines private sector risk-management methods with the tools and processes which the US intelligence services have used for decades, especially SATs (see below), to help filter out the emotions and biases that work against objective analysis.

Figure 1 below shows the overall flow of *Intelligent Analysis.* Note that the consumer is the beginning and end of the cycle that begins again at the starting point with follow-on requirements and questions. Subsequent chapters map to each step of the *Intelligent Analysis process.*

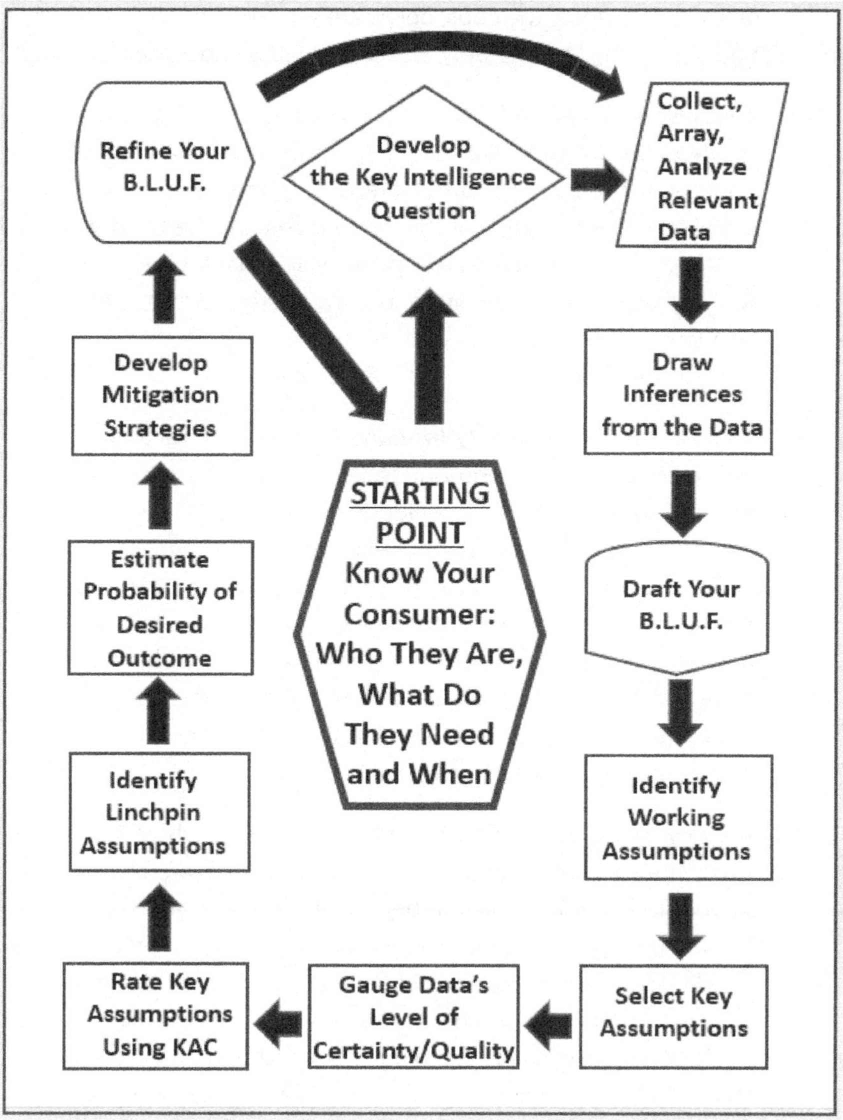

Figure 1. The flow of *Intelligent Analysis*; it maps to the chapters.

Unpacking *Intelligent Analysis*: Key Concepts Frame the Process

As you start to navigate the book, below are some of the key qualities that underpin our approach. Most notably, *Intelligent Analysis* does the following:

- ***Defines analyst broadly.*** For us the most important distinction is what you do with data—any data—you have collected. If you stop at this point you are just reporting on a topic. You become an analyst in name and practice if you analyze the data to show changes in trends and patterns that are the basis for looking ahead (the "so what") and draw inferences from what you see in the data. Then your action becomes intelligence analysis. Our book can help you make that leap.

- ***Defines consumer equally broadly.*** The standard dictionary definition is a person who purchases goods and services for personal use. For the US intelligence services, end-user consumers are policy makers and military leaders. But for us, consumers are the end-users of your analysis. In private and public sector organizations and law enforcement, consumers are generally clearly defined. It might be more difficult in other settings. For example, in academia it might be an instructor or dissertation adviser or the head of a lab. For authors, like us, it is our target audience. More of this in Chapter 2.

- ***Puts consumers first.*** Simply said, regardless of where they sit or their title, consumers of *Intelligent Analysis* are always your prime target. Following the opening exercise at the end of Chapter 3 you will choose a consumer as the end user who needs the analytic product you propose. You will write to what they need, delivered on time the same way. As the flow chart in Figure 1 shows, understanding them and what they need from you is the beginning, end, and beginning again of your work. A close colleague had this to say about the cost of thinking otherwise.

  "Consumers are busy and smart. They display great confidence in their own judgment. They can turn to many sources of information and often

come with strongly held views. Consumers generally do not need more information as much as they need help in making sense of the information they have." (Petersen, 2011)

- ***Makes extensive use of SATs.*** SATs are a suite of qualitative frameworks that rely on data-driven, structured discussions to help mitigate the impact of biases, emotions, and mindsets that work against objective analysis. We use SATs in each chapter to break down the analytic process into manageable steps toward developing each sentence of the B.L.U.F. Some of the SATs we use have long histories across the US intelligence services, but others we developed specifically for *Intelligent Analysis* to help guide analysts through each step in the process. Chapter 1 provides an in-depth discussion of SATs.

- ***Helps sustain momentum when drafting.*** The upfront work we require before you start to write gives you a clear roadmap to follow that can keep you on track. Our step-by-step process can help avoid a sense of drift when drafting. By this we mean that sense of being stuck when the story wavers and you are uncertain of what is next or simply when you have lost your focus.

- ***Avoids evaluating decision-making processes.*** *Intelligent Analysis* works like an X-ray—it reveals strengths and/or weaknesses of a decision that are not immediately apparent. So we focus only on validating the caveat (*likely, probably, unlikely*) used to estimate the probability that consumers will reach their desired state or an event or development will take place, not the decision-making process itself.

- ***Can play a similar role in data analytics.*** *Intelligent Analysis* can be used to test assumptions and develop prompts that, for example, may be important in shaping the right questions to ask.

- ***Embeds core values in how the analysis is done.*** The core values are written in stone and have been part of the DNA of the US intelligence services for decades. The two most important are:

***Value 1: Objectivity* is non-negotiable.** Analysts never bend to politics or avoid telling truth to power. Deliberately ignoring relevant data, skewing data, or excluding other perspectives makes the analysis suspect; those errors are easily spotted and violate analysts' fundamental value: their integrity. If tempted to cross that line, know that doing so puts your consumers and their organization's mission at risk. You would be better finding another line of work.

Value 2: *The consumer's agenda drives the process.* As noted above, the intelligence cycle underscores that the consumer must be the start and end points for *Intelligent Analysis*. At the end of Chapter 3 you will select the consumer—the targeted end user—of your product.

A corollary. To be clear, our central focus on consumers means that *Intelligent Analysis* always delivers that message in the B.L.U.F., which we complete at the end of Chapter 11. It leads every intelligence product and gives your consumer a complete analytic message. It is the product of really hard thinking that must be done before the first word is written. Once completed it can stand alone or be easily expanded into products of any length. We address each of the B.L.U.F.'s eight elements in subsequent separate chapters.

Because of the B.L.U.F.'s importance we want to introduce these elements below. The sequence and the format are fixed. Note how the B.L.U.F. moves consumers from what's known to what's next and the implications for consumers.

The B.LU.F. moves from <u>what's known</u> . . .

1. ***What?*** What development or event has prompted the consumer's question?
2. ***Why now?*** What is precipitating the event or development?
3. ***How does it work?*** Is there a process or terminology to be explained?
4. ***What is the impact so far?*** What has happened because of the event?

. . . . *to <u>what's next:</u>*

5. ***What is ahead?*** What is the "so what," the most likely outcome for the consumer, which includes an estimated level of probability that they will achieve their desired outcome or an event or development will occur.

6. ***What are the implications?*** What is "the so what of the so what" that explains the importance of what is ahead for your consumer over the near and longer term. It answers the question: What am I missing?
7. ***What can be done to mitigate risks?*** Steps can be taken to reinforce the strengths of an assessment or increase the likelihood of reaching the desired state by addressing key vulnerabilities.
8. ***Indicators of mitigation strategies' effectiveness.*** These are continuously collected data that measure their impact on the likelihood the consumer will reach their desired state or an event or development will take place.

Without a clearly thought-out and written B.L.U.F., analysts risk becoming overwhelmed with information and with no clear sense of how to start, or what to say, or how to avoid getting stuck. At best, in these circumstances their message becomes muddled and analysts wonder what happens when they, or their managers, go to review the text and try to figure out how it went off the track. In fact, each product has a shelf life of about thirty seconds. That is the time it takes for consumers to read the title and lead sentence to determine if the analysis answers their question with actionable intelligence. And if it falls short there may well not be a second chance.

What You Will learn

We focus on explaining and then practicing crafting each B.L.U.F. element using a series of structured techniques that will enable you to better:

- Understand the qualities of good intelligence and core values integral to the work
- Identify and manage biases that cloud objectivity and undermine collaboration
- Understand the role of assumptions in estimating probability
- Clearly identify your target audience, their challenges and issues
- Develop their KIQ focused on the problem they need solved
- Collect, analyze, and array data that answers the KIQ

- Convey the answer in the lead paragraph, the B.L.U.F.
- Systematically estimate the probability that your audience will reach their desired goal or an event or development will occur

Chapter Flow Builds Your B.L.U.F.

Each of our eleven chapters is a step in the *Intelligent Analysis* process. Again, it is based on your own work or project (or assigned depending on setting) and is aimed at a consumer selected at the end of Chapter 3. If up to you, it can be a product that is planned (alone or in a group), in progress, or already completed. If none of these are available, you could choose a consumer within your organization or academic program and develop a project around their assessed requirements.

The key is to work through the process. Exercises at the end of each chapter help you apply the lesson to your project.

- Chapters 1 through 4 focus on developing what's known, including an in-depth explanation of SATs, building deep understanding of consumers' operating environments and requirements, developing their KIQ, collecting data, and conducting an analysis that answers the question.
- Chapters 5 through 10 move analysts from what's known to what's next, including understanding how inferences express the KIQ's answer and bridge from what's known to what's next, drafting a B.L.U.F. that conveys the answer to the consumer, and developing a look-ahead that includes the estimated likelihood that consumers will achieve their desired outcome and mitigation strategies to improve outcomes.
- Chapter 11 provides guidance and practice related to drafting longer pieces, developing a summary, and reviewing your work.

Appendices include a template that can be used to plan a product (a version in Word is in the Workbook) and a more detailed glossary of key terms.

A Few Final Points

- *Intelligent Analysis* is ideal for groups, but it can be done with another colleague. Working alone, you would benefit from peer review of your work.
- The chapters build on each other, so read them and do the exercises in order.
- Do not skip steps. The cascading effect of missed exercises means a failed product.
- There are no correct answers to the exercises—just use your own work. If you follow the models and do the exercises, you will be fine.
- Finally, the analytic tradecraft so central to *Intelligent Analysis* is not a silver bullet, but you will learn how it can reduce the likelihood of errors and lead your shift from a collector of data to the world of practicing analysts.

Note: All exercises are to be completed in the Workbook, a downloadable MS Word document which is available by sending an email request to: **MakeEveryWordCount.2024@gmail.com.**

CHAPTER ONE

Build Your Foundation

> **"Weaknesses and biases inherent in human thinking processes . . . can be alleviated by conscious application of tools and techniques."**
>
> **"SATs are the process by which collaboration becomes most effective."**
>
> —Richards J. Heuer, *Psychology of Intelligence Analysis*

GOAL: To introduce key elements of *Intelligent Analysis*: SATs, recognized standards for delivering analytic products, the three key concepts central to crafting the look-ahead, and criteria for selecting a product to develop that meets a known consumer's intelligence questions.

Key Learning Objectives

At the end of this chapter, analysts will be better able to:

- Understand how *Intelligent Analysis* uses SATs to plan and structure objective data-driven analysis.
- Recognize how emotions and biases interfere with objective analysis.
- Explain the US intelligence community's standards that set the criteria for well-crafted products.
- Understand three key concepts that will be described in detail later in the book and are essential to determining the most likely outcome, probability, inferences, and assumptions.

In addition, the chapter:

- Introduces the application scenario that we use throughout the book as an example of how an intelligence product evolves at each step.
- Asks you to select a topic that you will work on and sets up Chapters 2 and 3, in which you will think about your consumer, their requirements, and the question they need to be answered, and then you will begin to select your target for the remainder of the book.

SATs Drive *Intelligent Analysis*

To start: a reminder and some background.

SATs are a suite of qualitative frameworks that rely on structured discussions to help mitigate the adverse impact of biases, emotions, and mindsets on objective analysis (more on this below). We use both well-known SATs and those which we developed as templates to provide an easy-to-follow model of each step.

Understanding the utility of SATs is key to testing a judgment's estimated level of probability (e.g., *likely, unlikely, probably, chances about even*) that the desired outcome will be achieved or an event or development will occur). SATs are especially important when making decisions in high-risk and uncertain operating environments with limited information. To deepen your understanding of SATs ahead of working through this and subsequent chapters, we recommend that you read or review *A Tradecraft Primer: Structured Analytic Techniques for Improving Intelligence Analysis*, published online by the US government in 2009. Heuer's first four chapters in *The Psychology of Intelligence Analysis* are also fundamental (Davis 1997; Heuer 1999; US Government 2002).

In addition to mitigating obstacles to objective analysis, SATs:

- ***Slow everyone down.*** Analysts are hardwired to make judgments, often focusing on meeting deadlines and, for multiple reasons, coming to closure too quickly, which leaves their analysis vulnerable to biases and emotions and their own expertise rather than hard data. SATs push analysts, working alone or in groups, to be more deliberate and conscious about how they arrive at their assessment.

- ***Encourage data-driven assessments.*** SATs expose unstated assumptions and group-think that can derail discussions and discourage dissent.

- ***Foster collaboration.*** In our approach, developing each B.L.U.F. element is based on group discussions that help keep the focus on the data, not each other. This structure helps ensure that everyone has a voice, more effectively leverages expertise, and integrates multiple viewpoints.

- ***Strengthen assessments' credibility.*** Stakeholders who are skeptical of the process or who are dug into their positions can at least see a transparent, defensible argument and inclusive process (US Government 2009).

EXERCISE: Meet Your Collaboration Challenge

One of SATs' important strengths is how effectively structured data-driven discussions can foster collaboration. Understanding collaboration challenges is the first step to overcoming them. Think about a past, current or prospective collaboration challenge in your own professional life.

Instructions:

Go to Chapter 1 in the Workbook and enter your responses there. This exercise can help you become more deliberate in defining any potential roadblocks you foresee in moving your own analytic product forward. The questions are below:

1. Detail the issue: What is the collaboration challenge?
2. What is blocking collaboration? Here, point out the specific issue.
3. What SATs might prove most useful? (Refer to US Government 2009)
4. Who needs to be at the table to solve this problem? Be specific.
5. Would outside experts be helpful?
6. What expertise might be missing or would add another perspective?

SATs Mitigate the Impact of Biases and Emotions on Objectivity

Analysts often turn to SATs at critical moments in the analytic process, especially when they find themselves bogged down, operating under pressure from widely divergent interpretations of limited information, or when emotions and biases usurp data-driven discussions. The chart below is drawn from Heuer's book. It points out the biases that pose the most serious risks to objective analysis.

PERCEPTUAL BIASES

- **Expectations.** We tend to perceive what we expect to perceive.
- **Resistance.** Perceptions resist change even in the face of new evidence.
- **Ambiguities.** Initial exposure to ambiguous or blurred stimuli interferes with accurate perception, even after more and better information becomes available.

BIASES IN EVALUATING EVIDENCE

- **Consistency.** Conclusions from a small body of consistent data engender more confidence than those drawn from a larger body of less consistent data.
- **Missing Information.** It is difficult to judge the potential impact of missing evidence, even if the information gap is known.
- **Discredited Evidence.** Even evidence proven wrong may not be sufficient to change perceptions quickly.

BIASES IN ESTIMATING PROBABILITIES

- **Availability.** Probability estimates are influenced by how easily we can image or recall similar instances.
- **Anchoring.** Probability estimates are adjusted only incrementally.
- **Overconfidence.** In determining levels of certainty, we are often overconfident, especially experts.

BIASES IN PERCEIVING CAUSALITY

- **Rationality.** Randomness, accident and error tend to be rejected as explanations for observed events.
- **Attribution.** Behavior of others is attributed to some fixed nature of the person or country, while our own behavior is attributed to the situation in which we find ourselves.

Figure 2. Heuer's recognized biases that undermine objective analysis.

In brief, we find that the term "Blind Spots" is another way to sum up Heuer's main biases. And we label ignoring or, more commonly dismissing them, as "Blind Spot Denial," where analysts simply refuse to recognize or admit they have them. We will see in Chapter 10 how consumers, despite the soundness of an analytic product or the consequences, simply cannot admit to or acknowledge them.

Premortems Look Back to Look Forward: Another Approach to Managing Biases

Premortems were developed after Heuer's book and have become another important diagnostic tool to help groups avoid bad outcomes. Most readers have at least heard the term *postmortem*, which refers to looking back at an event to determine what went wrong and why. In a well-run postmortem, a group can usually sort out what went well and point to systemic shortfalls. Because they are looking back at the history of the failure, however, there is a tendency to find blame that can send participants into a defensive posture. These behaviors can sideline quiet or less senior members who may have useful insights to add in answering the problem.

That said, what often surfaces in postmortems are problems that, if known and addressed ahead of time, could have altered the outcome. By contrast, in 2007 in *Harvard Business Review*, Gary Klein made this point: an assessment done before the launch of a product or decision-making process could also uncover these same vulnerabilities, thereby improving the chances for success (Klein 2007). We look ahead by looking backward. To paraphrase Nobel laureate Daniel Kahneman, who explained premortems in a 2014 video on YouTube (Premortem, 2014): before the launch of an initiative (product, experiment, merger, etc.), imagine a year down the road that an event derails the product. Write the hypothetical history of that disaster.

This illustrates the difference between postmortems and premortems:

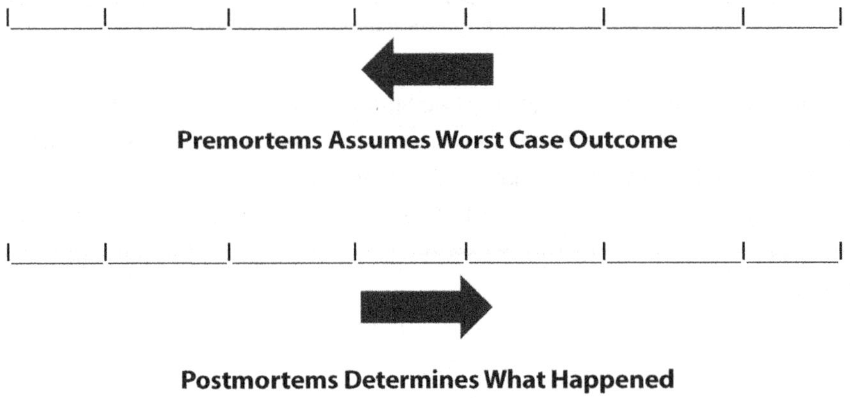

Figure 3. Premortems are proactive; postmortems look for blame.

In his YouTube video, Kahneman went further, asserting that premortems are the only effective way to look ahead because they focus only on what could go wrong, not on who did it. One of his most important points is that a properly run premortem encourages dissent and broad participation in a comparatively risk-free environment. To this end, premortems have been widely adopted across disciplines and business areas. For example:

- In the military they are used to plan operations.
- Hospitals have used premortem checklists that have led to major reductions in the spread of infection and improvements in surgery procedures.
- In France, premortems practiced twice yearly assumed there would be a fire in Notre Dame cathedral; these fire drills prepared first responders to head for the most valuable objects to rescue when the fire occurred.
- Banking regulators endorse the use of "reverse stress tests," in which a bank identifies a credible but unlikely failure scenario and demonstrates how well prepared the bank is to survive it.

Self-Assessments Uncover Biases, Reinforce Objectivity and Empower Analysts

Understanding how you mentally process information and manage yourself in daily interactions positions you to protect your own objectivity when working alone, as well as with other analysts more broadly. This book makes the case that the tools and processes of *Intelligent Analysis*, specifically how we use SATs, offer important safeguards against personal biases that often undermine objectivity. Adding a layer of self-awareness, however, can give you another tool that can serve as a mental check on the tradecraft, the proverbial X-ray that we mentioned in the Introduction. In addition, over time the combination of sound tradecraft and self-awareness can enable you to spot and help manage challenging group dynamics in a way that mitigates the biases and emotions that can impact objectivity.

Intelligence training courses often include personality assessments, which can also be self-administered. You may already be familiar with the two most widely used assessments cited below. If so, a retest might be useful to mark any change over time, and for first timers the scores can create a baseline. Both are available online and often free.

- **Myers-Briggs Type Indicator®.** An introspective self-report questionnaire that can help you gain insights about how you work and learn. For analysts, it is useful in understanding how you process information and make decisions.
- **Dominance, Influence, Steadiness, and Compliance (DISC©).** An assessment tool that can help you understand your behavior in the workplace; it is built around four distinct behaviors. It is free online and there are lots of videos that explain the results.

Of course, pros and cons of any self-assessment instrument abound, but even if you question their efficacy, taking them and interpreting the results can at least raise awareness of potential landmines on the road to objective analysis, whether working on your own or in a group

Well-Validated Quality Standards Define *Intelligent Analysis* and Frame the B.L.U.F.

Intelligent Analysis adheres to the same standards for drafting all analytic products that US intelligence services have followed for years. First formalized in the mid-1990s they became the core of the CIA's Sherman Kent School for Intelligence Analysis. Over the years other US intelligence agencies adopted them and they eventually migrated to counterpart organizations around the world.

The Office of Director of National Intelligence (ODNI) made the standards central to intelligence training across the US intelligence community and added to them as required. The ODNI initially memorialized them in 2007 and updated them in 2015. They apply to written assessments, oral/video presentations, and, more recently, graphics. Even as these standards have evolved, the core principles have remained unchanged and underpin every page of this and our first book:

- Assessments are customer-driven, objective, independent, timely and based on all relevant information sources
- Judgments and assessments are accurate, clear and logical

- Sources, data and methodologies are clearly explained
- Uncertainties are quantified according to a uniform scale

Three Concepts Shape How We Look Ahead

Looking ahead at the most likely outcome is a process rooted in facts ("what's known"). No guessing, predicting, or forecasting. And offering opinions that go beyond the data make you a pundit—not an analyst—and threaten your credibility. The concepts defined and briefly explained below are all of a piece, woven into how *Intelligent Analysis* moves from what's known to what's ahead, as we earlier showed in how the B.L.U.F. paragraph flows. First mentioned in the Key Terms, we explain them now because they are used frequently in the first chapters.

The three closely related terms explained below are inferences, estimated level of probability, and assumptions.

Inference. This term is an expression of what can be inferred about what's next from facts as known at the time of drafting and subject to change with new information. Here is the construct:

> Fact A + Fact B → C
> (→) is the symbol for implies, expressed in the caveat (likely, highly likely, probably, unlikely, etc.…). "C" is what can be inferred at the estimated likelihood.
>
> Here is an example:
>
> (A) The house is well built + (B) the interior spaces fit our needs → (implies C, what can be inferred) so we are likely (or highly likely) to buy it.

Estimated level of probability. The use of *likely* above is an example of a caveat. It expresses the estimated probability (estimated based on the facts) whether the desired outcome will be reached (e.g., a suitable house is purchased) or an event or development will take place based on what is known. The use of caveats is explored in much depth later. Other caveats include *unlikely, probably, highly unlikely*, terms that the US intelligence services have used for decades to tell consumers how close the analysts assess the inference to be accepted as a fact. For example: The house is well built + (B) the interior spaces fit our needs → (implies C, what can be inferred) so we will buy it. In this instance there is a range of reliable information about the house, builder, quality of the construction, and the design, so it is a good bet. Less reliable information and issues with the builder would change will to a caveat that expresses less certainty (*about even, or probably, or even unlikely*).

To be clear, looking at these terms explains your most important role as a practicing or aspiring analyst: to learn how to use the tools of *Intelligent Analysis*—the tradecraft—to assess whether the facts (A + B) support the implied (→) relationship (likely, unlikely...) with C (what can be inferred).

Assumptions. For the purposes of this book assumptions are conditions that must persist to support the estimated level of probability that the consumer will reach their desired outcome or an event or development will occur. That expressed likelihood of what is ahead must be subject to change with new information. The term "variable" is often used interchangeably but is more closely tied to economics and math.

Looking again at the hypothetical house purchase, examples of conditions that must hold to support the high level of certainty (*will*) might include that the prospective purchaser:

- Qualifies for financing
- Finds a lender and acceptable terms
- Sells their current home at the price they need
- Knows that the builder has a strong track record of building well-constructed homes

If, after the initial decision to buy the home, new data point to a weak real estate market or the buyer's credit score is too low, at least two of the buyer's conditions for completing the purchase are not holding up. In this case, *likely* to purchase might well become *unlikely* to purchase unless the two conditions can be addressed.

One more point about assumptions: they are the root of all arguments among analysts, and everyone else for that matter and just as often without even being aware they are assumptions. Biases and emotions can spark often heated and prolonged arguments over which caveat best expresses what can be inferred from the same set of facts. Consider the home buyer one more time. For those conditions to hold, the data had to support the estimated likelihood of a purchase as *likely*. Differences over the reliability of the data and how to interpret the impact of the data on the purchase decision are shaped by biases and emotions—think about the emotional charge of walking away from a house. Arguments over the impact of newly arriving information on the estimated probability can be even more contentious. We examine this dynamic in depth in Chapter 10.

The Application Scenario Illustrates Each Step in our Analytic Process

Below is the application scenario mentioned in the Introduction, which we will use as a continuous example of the methods described in the following chapters.

Brighton Precision Milling (BPM) Weighs Risks to Intellectual Property in Southeast Asian Expansion

To illustrate our approach more clearly, each chapter sets out another step in the process as we follow BPM's internal strategic planning discussions. The Board of Directors and senior managers are considering their first major investment outside the US in a country in Southeast Asia. The Board of Directors includes five founding shareholders with significant stakes in the company. BPM is a high-end milling company managing extensive supplier contracts with the US government and the automobile industry. The risks and rewards of expanding into Southeast Asia are substantial. The region is rife with rampant intellectual property theft and uneven law enforcement, but at the same time the company already has a presence there, and demand for its products is growing steadily.

For additional context, here is the US intelligence services' accepted definition of insider threat: "The threat that an employee will use their authorized access, intentionally or unintentionally, to do harm to the department's mission, resources, personnel, facilities, information, intellectual property, networks, or systems" (FBI, Guide, undated, UN Report on Southeast Asia; see also The National Insider Threat Task Force website (NITTF.gov).

Board of Directors and Senior Managers are Deeply Divided Over Risks

At issue are differences over BPM's ability to protect proprietary "G-codes" that control the movement of the cutting tools in their machines that could get hacked. BPM's machines consistently beat the competition in speed, accuracy, and quality. The G-codes potentially could be altered to make defective parts or used to start rival companies, or a competitor could use the codes to improve their performance (El Nabawi 2020).

NOTE: Ahead of setting out the position of the Board of Directors and the senior managers, we want to acknowledge that the back and forth within and between the two groups in our depiction does not capture the reality of group dynamics that almost always characterize discussions around important decisions. Our point is the process and how SATs can help keep the focus on the data and not personalities. We do, however, address group dynamics in Chapter 10, which includes suggestions on how best to keep the decision-making process on track.

The Board of Directors see the expansion as critical to the long-term growth of the company and to shareholders. They staked out their position in a memo to the senior managers:

> "Based on our review of Brighton Steel's insider threat program and its record of successfully detecting and thwarting multiple threats against our intellectual property, we assess that, working with a local partner, BPM is *highly likely* to manage the risks associated with opening and operating a plant in Southeast Asia, although a careful review of the operating environment will be required before moving forward."

The senior managers disagree. In addition to the G-codes, they are concerned about effectively managing a plant so far from home base over the long term. Senior managers expressed their views and welcomed the Board of Directors' willingness to review its highly optimistic assessment again. Both groups agreed to establish a short-term Task Force to evaluate the Board of Director's assessment. They brought in a facilitator practiced in the use (coincidentally) of *Intelligent Analysis*. The Task Force was drawn from the company's small but experienced intelligence and security staff and counterparts from the various divisions, including design, marketing, logistics, R&D, and in-house and outside counsel. The Task Force also included at least one outside expert from law enforcement. The Task Force's immediate consumers are the senior managers who support their consumers, the Board of Directors. Back to this later.

Before moving ahead we ask that you now select the analytic product you want to work on. The Task Force's decision can be a model.

EXAMPLE: BPM Task Force Defines Its Analytic Product

Below are the questions the Task Force answered in defining their analytic product.

What is the topic of your product?

- Who are your two consumers; who needs the analysis to act? Be specific by name or position; hit the right level—who needs to act?
- Why does it matter to each of your consumers; what makes it actionable?

What is the topic of the product?

- The product will focus on a high-stakes decision which BPM is making to open a plant in Southeast Asia and still protect its valuable intellectual property.

Who is/are the consumer(s)?

- Name two. Be specific by name or position: who needs the actionable intelligence you will produce.
- For the BPM Task Force, the two consumers are the senior managers and their consumers the Board of Directors. Again, both are consumers of the analysis.

Why does it matter to them?

- This will be BPM's first effort to expand its reach outside the US, and the senior managers and Board of Directors differ over whether to make the move.

EXERCISE: Choose Your Two Potential Consumers and Your Product to Support Them

Instructions:

Turn to Chapter 1 in the Workbook.

First, think about the analytic product that you want to build. Ideally, it should be work planned or in progress. If you wish you can use an already completed product to take through the process. Regardless, it needs to deliver actionable intelligence.

Second, select two potential consumers. One should be a consumer you currently support, and the second might be someone you would like to support but have not yet worked with. You will choose one at the end of Chapter 3.

> **Note:** It may well be that at this point you are hard pressed to decide what you want to write and for whom. If you already have an idea or an already completed project, fine. If not, please be careful to make sure that what you choose is targeted at the right level by name or position, has lots of available data, and has clear potential consumers for your product. We would suggest a professor, a panel, report on an experiment, or a local issue. On the latter, please look no higher than the county or state level for your consumer. Beyond that may find you hard pressed to develop a targeted product.

LAST STEP: Advice Before Moving On

To shift from laying the foundation of *Intelligent Analysis* to actually doing the work, let's revisit one of my favorite quotes that helps remind you of what we are about.

> ***"Thinking analytically is a skill like carpentry or driving a car. It can be taught, it can be learned, and it can improve with practice."***
> —Richards Heuer, *The Psychology of Intelligence Analysis*

As we said in the preface, we agree with Heuer's point.

The skills for developing analytic products regardless of where you work or what you do are accessible to anyone interested in learning them. Think of *Intelligent Analysis* as "rearranging neurons" in your brain or helping you by looking through different lenses.

The ability and desire to do well are already there or you would not have bought our book. *Intelligent Analysis* just gives analysts the structure and process to become more conscious and deliberate as they develop their products, both critical traits of good analysts.

Intelligent Analysis requires no permission to implement. Participants in our courses often express concerns that our format is inconsistent with organizational requirements or, worse, that the culture is resistant to change. But regardless of the format, the analysis—the thinking—will fit and will be transparent to reviewers.

Practice and diligently complete every step. It is that simple: do the work, learn the craft, and practice. Confidence will follow. Find joy in the work, it makes excelling easier. (On tradecraft see Davis 1997; Gartin 2019; Petersen 2011; Pfeffer and Sutton 2006; Taleb 2008.)

CHAPTER TWO

Know Your Consumer

> **"Every intelligence product must be rooted in a strong understanding of the consumer it is written for."**
>
> —Martin Petersen, *What I Learned in 40 Years of Doing Intelligence Analysis for US Foreign Policymakers* (Studies)

GOAL: To better understand why expertise, knowledge of the consumer, and a service mentality are essential to building the trust that will determine the strength of the consumer-analyst relationship.

Key Learning Objectives

At the end of this chapter, analysts will be better able to:

- Explain how trust fuels the strength of consumer-analyst relationships.
- Understand that it is the analyst's responsibility to help build those relationships.
- Demonstrate the use of our first two SATs that help you understand consumers' worlds and how you can probe more deeply into what they need from you and what their intelligence requirements are.

Consumers' Trust Fuels *Intelligent Analysis*

The relationship between consumers and analysts is the start and end point of *Intelligent Analysis* and then the starting point again. One way to think about this relationship is to see yourself as your consumer's eyes and ears, functioning as a trip wire, identifying data that, for better or worse, impacts their immediate agendas or points to a trend on the horizon that could affect the organization. When analysts provide that support, they are in the room or on the plane with consumers even if analysts never meet them. Analysts' assessments speak for themselves. There are few second chances.

Underlying the pressure on analysts to produce consistently objective, well-documented assessments is the consumer's vulnerability to your mistakes, because you are essentially asking them to trust you and your tradecraft. They are counting on your professionalism and integrity to protect them, to make them successful. The stake in these relationships is what makes *Intelligent Analysis* so important. Our approach means that consumers can expect the assessments to be tightly focused on their requirements and timed to support their schedules. The analysts' work is complete, objective, data-driven, and clearly written the same way every time.

Two Frameworks Sharpen Consumer Focus

Understanding your consumers' operating environment—the world they must manage every day—and what they need from you are central to meeting these high standards. Specifically, you must identify who you are writing for by name and/or position and know exactly what they need from you, when, and in what format. No guesses or writing what you think they need. Doing this homework helps analysts become more proactive, relevant, and mission focused. Ignorance of these essentials leaves analysts and consumers sidelined and unhappy.

Intelligent Analysis offers two SATs that will help analysts assess what they know and do not know about their consumers' day-to-day operating environment. You will find that while two consumers may start with the same data, they see the same development or event from different perspectives, which means they will each have different intelligence requirements. But only theirs matters to them.

The chart below provides an example of a completed framework which focuses on BPM's internal discussions. Note that both look at the same issue but from very different perspectives that underscore this point. Explanations of the columns are below the framework.

EXAMPLE: Complete the Consumer Identification Framework

1. Identify consumers.	2. To whom does consumer report?	3. What is their day like?	4. What are their most important concerns?	5. How much do they know about analysts?
BPM Board of Directors	- Shareholders	- BPM is part time job - Intense focus on shareholder value	- Representing shareholders' interests - Company decision making	The founders say they have some knowledge; other members indicate very little
Senior BPM managers	- Board of Directors	Multitask: - Meetings - Business decisions - Staffing - Expanding the market - Profit margins	- Market share - Stay ahead of competition - Surprises	Generally familiar with who they are and what they do; trust them to be on task force

Figure 4. Same development, different perspectives, and operating environments

Explanation of the columns starts with Column 1.

- *Column 1:* Specifically, who can act on the analyst's assessment?
- *Column 2:* To whom does the consumer report? In many instances, what analysts provide consumers is destined for the person they report to. For example, the assessment may feed into a larger product or oral briefing for a more senior consumer. If so, the key here is to be sure you know how to help the primary consumer be successful as the analysis moves up the management chain.
- *Column 3:* What is their day like? Obviously, they are busy, but busy with what specifically? For example, do they have time to

read reports, sort through data, and set priorities, or is most of their day scheduled or unpredictable?

- *Column 4:* What are their most important concerns? What do they worry most about? Typically, they worry about surprises, risks to personnel, unwelcome publicity, an unexpected event, or being blindsided.
- *Column 5:* How much does the consumer know about analysts? Typically not much, unless the target consumer is among the few that come to their position with some exposure to the value analysts can add.

This last item offers the analyst both a challenge and opportunity. "Analyst" to some consumers may well be a vague term that conjures up a fortune teller capable of predicting what is next. And they are highly unlikely to understand that analysts practice a unique skill set. They might even identify analysts as academics or extra hands to be used as needed. If this is the case, you and your management should plan sessions where you learn about how much they know about analysis and what it can offer and start to build that trust that will be so important. You can explain who you are and what you do and find out what they need from you, and then stay in contact to update their agendas and requirements (Wilder 2011).

EXERCISE: Complete the Consumer Identification Framework

Identify Your Target Consumers: Who Do You Want to Take Action?

Instructions:
Turn to Chapter 2 in your Workbook.

Complete the Consumer Identification Framework, specifically, who needs to act? Recall that the first consumer should be one you are supporting now and the second is a consumer who would benefit from your product whom you are not currently supporting.

Complete the Consumer Identification Framework for both your potential consumers. You will choose only one of them at the end of Chapter 3 to use throughout the rest of the exercises. Leave blank what is unknown—do not guess. Filling in the blanks is part of the exercise.

Assess Consumers' Intelligence Requirements: What Do they Need From You?

Knowing what actionable intelligence the consumer needs is the second half of the analyst's task. Figure 5 below shows the framework that, when completed, will confirm the consumers' near- and long-term priority intelligence requirements. These requirements must be updated regularly with your consumer's (or their staff's) assistance, sometimes as often as weekly, to make sure analysts are focused on what matters and on the timing. Again, note that one development prompts interest from multiple consumers.

Specifics about their requirements will determine your focus. They may need, for example:

- An explanation of a development or event
- Assessment of competitors
- Market update
- An oral presentation
- Graphs or charts
- Potential long-term risks or opportunities
- A heads up about a near-term threat

The table below uses BPM as an example of an intelligence requirement assessment.

EXAMPLE: Complete the Consumer Requirements Assessment Framework

BPM's Consumer Requirements Assessment Framework

1) Identify Your Consumer(s): Who Do You Want to Act?	2) Summarize Your Consumer(s)' World.	3) Explain Your Consumer(s)' Highest Priority Issues.	4) Explain Your Consumer(s)' Long-Term Issues.	5) How Can I Learn More About These Consumer(s)?
BPM Board of Directors	- Service on multiple boards. - Intense focus on shareholders - Staying informed a challenge - Integrating new technology	- Open plant in SE Asia - Profit margins - Stock price - Fend off activist investors - Oversight of executive decisions	- Support strategic planning - Succession planning - Maintain independence - Prioritize investments	- For analysts: rely on senior managers, do your own out-reach, maybe watch their schedules
Senior BPM managers	- Swamped with meetings, personnel issues - Little time for planning - Filled with uncertainty	- Hire and retaining staff - Know the competition - Increase profit margins - Avoid surprises/ minimize uncertainty	- Prioritize investments - Productive relations with the Board of Directors - Look for new opportunities and vulnerabilities	The Task Force assessing the risk will have to collaborate with management to make certain they understand the requirements

Figure 5. Knowing requirements is the other half of the consumer knowledge equation.

Here is an explanation of columns 2–5:

- ***Columns 1 and 2:*** Summarize Your Consumer(s)' World. Should be based on analysts' responses in the Consumer Assessment Framework

- *Column 3:* What are the consumers' highest priority issues? Looking over the next thirty to sixty days, what are their most immediate requirements?
- *Column 4:* What are their long-term issues? What are their more strategic priorities with a horizon ranging from six months to a year and beyond?
- *Column 5:* How can I learn more about your consumer? Not a time to be shy. Use your supervisor and set up lunch or breaks with counterparts. Find out who knows the schedules and look for changes; this will position analysts to write to their agendas.

EXERCISE: Complete the Consumer Requirements Assessment Framework

Instructions:

Turn to Chapter 2 in the Workbook.

- For your project complete the requirements assessment framework for both potential consumers. Leave blank what is unknown. Be as specific as you can but do not guess. It is part of the exercise.
- Once again, note the differences between the two consumers as they look at the same event or development from their own perspectives.

1. Identify consumers.	2. To whom does consumer report?	3. What is their day like?	4. What are their most important concerns?	5. How much do they know about analysts?
Reenter from first exercise	Reenter from first exercise			
Reenter from first exercise	Reenter from first exercise			

We stress two key points to take away, First, multiple consumers looking at the same development will each look at it from their perspective, underscoring a point we make throughout the book that one size does not fit all. Second, it is not always easy to fill in the blanks in the frameworks, but guessing or assuming you understand what they need could mean missing the dynamic of operating environments and their changing requirements. The distance erodes the relationship. Staying engaged keeps you proactive in meeting their requirements: what they need, the timing, and the format. Trust is built and the work becomes rewarding.

CHAPTER THREE

Consumer Knowledge and Collaboration Shape Key Intelligence Question

GOAL: To develop the right Key Intelligence Question that targets the right issue at the right time to meet known near- or long-term requirements.

Key Learning Objectives

At the end of this chapter, analysts will be better able to:

- Explain the significance of the KIQ and why it is a collaborative process.
- Develop a strong KIQ and Sub-questions for your consumer using the Intelligence Question Refinery.
- Understand the serious risks that come when analysts assume they know what the consumer needs and then answer the question within the KIQ instead of the KIQ itself.
- Finally, select the target consumer you will work with throughout the rest of the exercises.

Develop the Right Key Intelligence Question at the Right Time

The right intelligence question flows from understanding the consumer's near- and long-term priorities. This knowledge and substantive expertise are the two essential ingredients in formulating a timely KIQ (Walton, Intelligence Question Refinery; Walton, Presentation). The third ingredient is collaboration between analysts and their consumers or their staff to make certain that the analytic product answers the right question at the right time. Why? Because everything from here on depends on it.

KIQs drive the analysts' work every day. And the KIQ can evolve as new data comes in so you may have to go back to the consumer to ensure it is still on target.

Finding the right question also means that analysts are able to understand and respond to questions about the same development from multiple consumers. This would certainly be the case with BPM's Task Force. In other instances, it can become more complicated when, as often is the case, a single analyst is covering a suddenly "hot" issue that engages multiple stakeholders.

The first question can be readily handled, but how does an analyst respond when, for example, four other department heads, including several unfamiliar to you, send their own questions on the same development to the same analyst ahead of an upcoming meeting? The good news is that your outreach skills have paid off. What is clear from the rush of pre-meeting questions, however, is that a "one-size" answer will not fit all. This means there is work first to clarify all stakeholders' requirements before drafting any responses. Attention to these issues now will help you avoid "firing blanks" later on.

Good Key Intelligence Questions Meet Strict Criteria

In looking for clarity from each stakeholder, the analyst knows that to be most helpful, each KIQ must:

- **Be open ended.** An open-ended question gives analysts the opportunity to provide a complete answer to the question with all of the B.L.U.F. elements. This approach can help steer analysts and the consumer away from simple yes or no answers. Yes or no questions are certainly valid and cannot be ignored, but generally there is something else they want to know, and an open question aims to get at something deeper. Analysts need to ask for clarification: what does the consumer really want to know?

    - For example, a car buyer wants a straightforward answer to the question: "Does this car run well?" Some follow-up questions, however, get at what the car buyer really wants to know: "What indications are there that this car will satisfy my driving expectations?" The answer to the first question is binary; the answer to the second invites a more comprehensive answer. Trying to help a consumer become more specific might be as simple as asking: "What problem are you trying to solve?"

    - "To what extent" questions work as well: "To what extent is the car a good purchase?" "To what extent is the car ready to drive?"

- **Be time-bound.** Create a time frame (near- or longer term) and make room for context and trend lines.
    - For example, a question such as: "What indications are there that the airline will improve its on-time record?" provides no time frame for the story. Adding "over the next 30 days" does the trick: it gives a look at near-time possibilities.
- **Be consumer-approved up front.** Forming the question is a collaborative process. Again, looking back at the questions thrown at analysts, make sure that the question reflects what needs to be answered, even if it feels uncomfortable going back to clarify what is really on their minds; it must be part of the process. It might be called "peeling back the layers of the issue." This approach has proven effective and welcome.
- **Must not answer the "question within the question."** This last standard merits a deeper look because of the potential impact on the analysis if it is ignored. For examples of a question within the question, look at the following:
    - Why is this bank involved in money laundering?
    - What makes this car manufacturer cheat on emissions tests?

Both questions are legitimate and based on indications of possible malfeasance. But a closer read shows that in both cases the questions assume the bank and car manufacturer are guilty. Read them again. The answers are predetermined. It is not that the bank and car manufacturer are not guilty, but rather that the questions pose a risk to analytic objectivity.

The ripple effect of these flawed KIQs begins with deciding what information to collect—i.e. cherry picking—and ends with an assessment that is incomplete and highly likely to be biased. This serious—we argue potentially fatal—failure of analytic tradecraft occurs when analysts believe themselves smarter than the consumer; they assume they know what their consumer needs or wants to hear. They are not.

Consider the impact of this assessment on unknowing consumers who assume you have done your job. To be clear, from our perspective this sort of arrogance is an abdication of analytic tradecraft with potentially serious consequences. If you cannot resist skipping this step you will fail as an analyst and you might consider another line of work.

EXERCISE: Turn these questions into good KIQs

Instructions:

Turn to Chapter 3 in the Workbook.

To practice applying the criteria, how would you recast the following questions?

For example:

Incorrect: "Did you see this morning's WSJ headline? Holy cow!!"
Correct: "To what extent will our investment be at risk over the next six months?"

Or

"What indicators have we seen that our investment will be at risk over the next six months?"

Now follow the pattern and make the fixes:

- "Will Acme beat our new widget to market?"
- "Competition is everywhere: are we vulnerable?"
- "How is Acme doing these days?"

The Intelligence Question Refinery Framework Helps Develop Tailored KIQs

To consistently formulate good KIQs, use the Intelligence Question Refinery. It has been well-validated among the US intelligence services that have used it for decades to help analysts be more deliberate in developing the right KIQ that meets consumers' requirements (Walton, Refinery). The framework might look straightforward, but it is often the analyst's most difficult challenge because it requires both analytic expertise and consumer knowledge, and because of the ever-present temptation to assume analysts already know what they need to know and the answer. Most notably, the refinery:

- **Drives a more deliberate process.** Breaking down the KIQ into sub-questions (see below) serves to counter the biases that can interfere with an assessment.

- **Broadens the response.** The refinery drives the rest of the *Intelligent Analysis* process, especially what data to collect, which so often stymies analysts.
- **Requires engagement with consumers.** With multiple consumers focused on the same development with different questions, the refinery helps articulate the differences.

EXAMPLE: The BPM Task Force Drafts a KIQ for their two consumers

The Board of Directors and seniors need to agree on their KIQ—what do they really want to know. They turn to the Task Force for a draft that tries to capture both perspectives based on their stated positions.

> **Note:** Recall that for this exercise only, we have returned to both the Task Force's two initial consumers—the senior managers and their consumers, the Board of Directors— to illustrate how different constituencies will arrive at different KIQs about the same development. Explanations of each column are below the refinery.

To remind you of where we are, recall that the senior managers and their consumers, the Board of Directors, are at odds over whether the company can establish a plant in Southeast Asia that will be able to secure its intellectual property--their proprietary G-codes—that run the milling machines. We will see in the chart below how their differences spill over into how they frame their KIQs. You will be asked to do the same plus a related exercise at the end of the chapter. The explanations of each column in the chart are below the refinery.

EXAMPLE: The Task Force's Draft Intelligence Question Refinery: Two Perspectives

Consumer	Development	Raw Question	Key Issue	Specific Consumer Interests	Time Frame	Refined Question
BPM Board of Directors	Potential for BPM to expand into Southeast Asia w/local partner	How can BPM expand into Southeast Asia?	How quickly can this be done?	The potential to increase profits and protect stakeholder interests	12–18 months to initiate	How quickly would a local partner be able to establish the plant and put in place a system to protect BPM's intellectual property?
Senior BPM Managers/ Analytic Task Force	Board of Directors' strong interest in expanding into Southeast Asia w/local partner	Why would we do this?	How does BPM benefit and how can it be managed?	Risk to intellectual property? How can it be managed?	2–3 years to initiate	To what extent is BPM positioned to expand into Southeast Asia in a way that can protect the company's intellectual property?

Figure 6. The Intelligence Question Refinery helps sort out differing consumer requirements about the same development.

Explanation of columns:

- *Column 1.* **The Consumers:** Listing both of them here clearly illustrates where the differences are in terms of what each consumer wants to know.
- *Column 2.* **Development:** Something just happened, and consumers ask, "What does this mean?"
- *Column 3.* **Raw Question:** This is an unrefined first reaction to the development: Is there any substance to this report?

- *Column 4.* **Key Issue:** What do analysts think is at the heart of the raw question?
- *Column 5.* **Specific Consumer Interests:** What is this consumer most concerned about currently? Each consumer is likely to have very different concerns. At this point, the question can become more tailored, but analysts still need the consumers' knowledge and input to refine the question.
- *Column 6.* **Time Frame:** How far do analysts need to look ahead? What is the planning horizon? This could differ widely as well because of the multiple requirements that must be met.
- *Column 7.* **Refined Question:** The refined questions in that last column meet the requirements of both groups looking at the same development. The Board of Director's question assumes a partner would be able to set up the plant AND would put in place a system to safeguard the intellectual property; it is all about stock value and short-term gains. It addresses only a narrow subset of the challenges each BPM division has to consider. It does not meet the criteria for a good intelligence question.
- In contrast the senior managers, our sole consumers from here on, have a much broader range of concerns. Their question underscores their long-term concerns. They reasoned that members of the Board of Directors change, but as managers they will end up dealing for years with the consequences of a poor decision.

Here is the final refined and approved KIQ:

- To what extent is BPM positioned to expand into Southeast Asia in a way that can protect the company's intellectual property?

Note why the approved KIQ meets the criteria. Most notably it is:

- **Open ended.** It does not lead to a predetermined answer and leaves room for a full response. Use of terms such as to what extent, what factors, what indicators, or how well help in that regard because the response could be at any point along a continuum, depending on the data.

- **Focused on the highest priority near-term issue.** Because developing the KIQ is a collaborative process, analysts can distinguish the KIQ from the consumers' other questions that may be important and need to be answered—*but not now.* (see below)

The key takeaway from the exercise is that "one size does not fit all." *Intelligent Analysis* requires a focus on the requirements of each consumer, which means understanding who they are and what they need from you. To be clear, going forward the senior managers are the Task Force's consumers. The senior managers have their own consumers—the Board of Directors.

EXAMPLE: Develop Sub-questions

Sub-questions are those that must be answered to respond to the refined KIQ. Specifically, Sub-questions break down the refined questions to facilitate a still more focused response. Based on the approved KIQ the Task Force's Sub-questions break down the approved refined question only for their consumer. The Board will review these as well.

The examples below illustrate possible Sub-questions the Task Force developed. The list could be considerably longer, perhaps as many as fifteen or twenty areas need to be explored. All the questions might be valid, but only those that must be answered to respond to the KIQ are included. The others can be addressed later in the follow-on products. Here are the Task Force's Sub-questions. Note that they still adhere to the correct formulation:

- What indications do we see that a local partner would serve our interests?

- To what extent will a suitable manufacturing facility be available?

- To what extent can the local labor market provide sufficiently skilled staff and management personnel?

- To what extent will the required raw materials be available locally?

- What indicators would tell us that the legal system in Southeast Asia would protect foreign investors and capital repatriation?
- To what extent are there locations outside Southeast Asia that would still bring us closer to the market?

Sub-questions serve several purposes:

- They quickly narrow down the data.
- Placed in the right order they can help structure the response.
- In a time crunch the questions can be divided among colleagues to answer (but make sure they know how they need to be answered in a B.L.U.F. format).

Knowing these other Sub-questions can help you draft a different set of KIQs that focus on what's next and target data collection to answer them. The other questions do not have to be answered now but can be the basis for follow-on pieces (with consumer approval). This "homework" also builds expertise and positions you to respond more quickly to new requirements.

EXERCISE: Develop the KIQ for Your Product

Instructions:
Turn to Chapter 3 in the Workbook.

Develop the KIQ for both potential consumers. Use BPM's example and complete the refinery or use the prompts below the framework. Getting this process right is key to the book's remaining exercises. Blank entries in any of the columns point out gaps in consumer knowledge that need to be filled. *Do not jump to the refined question; the stakes are too high to skip steps.* Again, note the differences: one development, multiple consumers, different perspectives, and KIQs.

Stop: before developing Sub-questions choose the consumer whom you are targeting with your product. Now restate the product you will be working on.

- What is your product?
- Specifically, who is your consumer by name and position?

- Why does it matter to your consumer; what makes it actionable?

Restate the KIQ you developed for your chosen consumer.

EXERCISE: Develop Sub-questions

Instructions:

Turn to Chapter 3 in the Workbook.

Only for the KIQ for your chosen consumer:

- List five or six Sub-questions that need to be answered to answer the KIQ.
- After listing them, select only those you must address to answer the refined KIQ.
- Arrange them in priority order.

Other Sub-questions may well be valid but you only care about those related directly to your KIQ. The others can be the basis for follow-on products.

Getting the KIQ Right Really Matters

For *Intelligent Analysis*, the refinery accomplishes two important goals:

- **It works against biases.** Even experienced analysts—because they think they are so smart, are confident (overly so in some instances), or because they think they know their consumer—may answer the "question in the question." Such biases can cause even more harm if the question fuels the consumers' predilections as well.
- **It can provide guidance for your long-term planning.** What you have taken away from the consumer assessment and KIQ exercises tells you specifically what issues preoccupy them.

To close, by following the practices in these last two chapters, analysts will have identified their target consumer, their requirements, and the KIQ that needs to be answered. Already that vast, intimidating pool of data has quickly become far more manageable. Now analysts are ready to gather the data to answer that known question.

CHAPTER FOUR

Collect, Array and Analyze Data

"Without data, you are just another person with an opinion."

—W. Edward Deming, Forbes, 2016

> **GOAL: To understand that data collected, arrayed, and analyzed is the starting point for producing data-driven *Intelligent Analysis* that answers the consumer's KIQ.**

Key Learning Objectives

At the end of this chapter, analysts will be better able to:

- Describe how consumer knowledge and the refined KIQ help you target the data that needs to be collected and analyzed to provide a data-driven response to the consumer's requirement.
- Develop a collection plan that includes what types of data and graphics would best answer your consumer's KIQ.
- Explain the importance of well-crafted graphics that help analyze how the data answers the KIQ.
- Complete the last two of the four B.L.U.F. elements that reflect your understanding of What's Known, as a bridge to What's Next.

In a separate exercise summarize your work so far, so that it serves as a bridge from What's Known to What's Next.

> **Hints:** To stay tightly focused on collecting only the data required to answer the agreed upon KIQ and Sub-questions, we have found that keeping the KIQ close at hand helps avoid being distracted by what is interesting but not relevant. The exercises begin after the section on developing graphics to array your data.

Data Fuels *Intelligent Analysis*

Start with data, every time.

To understand the centrality of data to *Intelligent Analysis*, recall the eight B.L.U.F. elements (defined in Chapter 1) that divide our approach between

What's Known and What's Next. We complete that shift at the end of this chapter with a summary exercise based on lessons learned in the first four chapters.

- Consumer knowledge and an approved KIQ (Chapter 3) provide the data needed to complete the B.L.U.F.'s first two elements—"what's the development" and "why now"—that more clearly define your project and the situation's time frame.

- Consumer knowledge and the KIQ also help analysts more efficiently and completely collect, analyze, and array the data that will underpin the last two components of what's known—"how does it work" and "the impact so far"—that are data-driven.

- Our application scenario later in the chapter shows how all four elements together constitute What's Known and set the stage for What's Next, the last four B.L.U.F. elements.

(This chapter draws on multiple sources—Davenport 2013; Pfeffer, McKinsey and Sutton 2006; Taleb 2008a; Taleb 2008b).

Up front we want to raise two critical points that underscore the importance of this chapter.

- First, dig. The data must answer the consumer's known and approved KIQ completely, indeed exhaustively. This is probably the most time-consuming part of the process, but it is critical in developing the most likely outcome and sustaining trust with your consumer as the assessment unfolds. Dig.

- Second, stay objective. Like a poorly formed or unapproved KIQ, narrowing or cherry-picking data collection (consciously or not) to support your analysis or your consumer's agenda poses a serious risk to your consumer. It will at some point be discovered. It is a serious breach of trust and will at best damage your credibility and at worst could well end your career as an analyst. Skewing collection to please a consumer will have the same outcome with potentially serious consequences.

The term data describes information found in two forms: quantitative and qualitative.

- ***Quantitative or digital*** data is numeric. It measures values expressed as numbers (how many, how much, how often, where) arrayed in tables or charts.

- ***Qualitative*** data is less precise because by definition it is non-numerical. This information is based on observations—data that can be observed and recorded—but also needs to be quantified to be useful and can be readily displayed alongside purely digital data to provide a broadly gauged response. This type of data is collected by observation, one-on-one interviews and focus groups, as well as open-source data (print, other media), comments on survey forms, or official reports or studies in hard or soft copy.

Initial data searches set a baseline (as-is state) that provides a near-term answer to the KIQ. Follow-on data collection marks any changes in trends, patterns, or relationships that need to be reported. Over time, data collection fuels long-term assessments.

EXAMPLE: Data-Driven Analysis Spots Emerging Threat and Deepens Understanding of What's Known

Here is a short scenario illustrating how both digital and qualitative data underpin actionable intelligence.

In this example, an analyst working in a law enforcement intelligence unit has tracked gang activity for the last six months, developing the as-is baseline assessment. The baseline showed that the gang's operating area had remained static, in large part because of an expected southeast area slowdown as colder weather quieted the streets. Over the weekend, however, two untested sources reported what appeared to be a known gang's efforts to expand its territory from the southeast into the northwest part of the city. The chart below illustrates how data shaped What's Known and drove the story that helped local law enforcement look at What's Next and keep them ahead of the gang's activities.

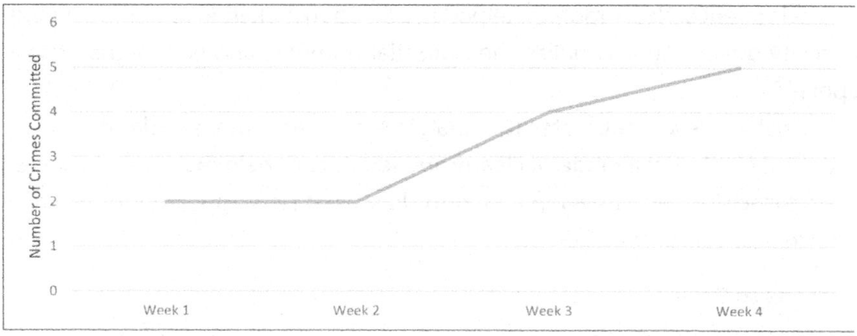

Figure 7. Possible change in as-is state in the NW quadrant January 2020.

The analyst, armed with the consumer's known questions, reported the anomaly and watched for more indications of the possible shift. Using quantitative data, the analyst started to build a series of tables and maps to track what was known about the possible changes, including locations of current activity and possible gang involvement. The data showed that the number of crimes held steady during the first two weeks of January. But a change in that pattern surfaced over the last two weeks of January. Police patrols provided qualitative reports from locals who observed an upturn in the number of low-level crimes. They also reported that the gang activity appeared to include unknown teenagers, a rarity in a tightly knit neighborhood.

For their part, the intelligence unit had a good handle on the neighborhood players. With that understanding of the as-is state, the analyst was able to confirm that those recently arrested were, in fact, previously unknown to police. The new faces and new gang markings pointed to a potential new pattern in gang activity that included interlopers from across town or even farther afield.

Over the next several weeks more data arrived enabling the analyst to update tables and maps with data from incoming crime reports and community residents' observations. Increased surveillance and officers' own observations further raised the likelihood that a new pattern was emerging. With that new data the analyst provided the new sources with more focused data collection. Other confidential sources and added patrols further fed the analysis.

With the stepped-up data collection, together with more interviews and meetings, the analyst in mid-February was able to assess that the new pattern "probably" meant that the shift was permanent. By late February the analyst increased the likelihood of a permanent change from "probably" to "very likely," which raised concerns about a spike in more serious crime and gang-on-gang related violence. New graphics helped the decision makers in law enforcement and city government visualize the potential numbers and early signs of "hot spots."

Finally, a few weeks later the analyst produced a more in-depth assessment that included a range of clearly arrayed data to help managers make resource decisions and develop a plan to slow what now appeared to be a real shift in that part of the city.

Lessons to Draw

Data Answers Two B.L.U.F. Elements: How It Works and Impact So Far

This scenario is consistent with the challenges all analysts face in spotting and reporting potentially important shifts from the current baseline understanding of an issue. The analyst clearly understood this requirement in raising the new reporting from untested sources. Note how carefully the analyst made that point. No opinion, no "gut instincts."

- **How it works.** Moving forward the analyst, again using the baseline, explained how the gangs had been operating and changing patterns of behavior. The analyst included both qualitative and quantitative data to show how the pattern change mapped to early indications of upticks in criminal activity in the new area.

- **Impact so far.** In the weeks ahead the analyst collected and analyzed more data that pointed to new "hot spots," movement of new players into the neighborhood, and police reports of growing community concerns.

Over time the combined data guided the stepped-up collection of information that provided stakeholders with the quantitative data needed to make resource allocation decisions.

Two More Points on Data Management

First, qualitative data needs to be quantified to be useful. Note how the analyst and police used qualitative—non-digital—data such as interviews and focus groups or anecdotal data to provide context, which reinforced digital data, provided a deeper look at the level of community concerns, and catalogued what residents had observed.

- Non-digital responses are called *categorical data*. Nonetheless, they must be quantified to be integrated into the analysis. For example, community residents might indicate that they have seen the gang operating mostly in the evenings, but more recently in the daytime as well.

Second, raise emerging threats early-on but be data-driven.

- Note that the analyst decided to report the first indications of the gang's potential shift even though it was based on new and untested sources because it could signal a change in the as-is state.

- We think this is the right approach. Analysts should raise an issue even if it is based on a sole report. Let the consumer decide how to use the report. Assuming that a new data point is just a single anomaly invites blindsiding your consumer.

Real World Experience: Early Warning Pays Off

Withholding incomplete or even questionable data from consumers on an event or development of high-priority interest can be self-defeating. Reporting What's Next—tomorrow or over the horizon--is the analyst's job. We have told analysts serving on sensitive accounts, especially in law and financial crimes enforcement settings, that as part of their warning function, one data point, yes *one data point*, is enough to note. It is not "crying wolf." Rather, the note should not be dashed off but properly sourced and drafted consistent with analytic tradecraft. Be sure to check databases to see if the new development has surfaced elsewhere—what you are seeing is unlikely to be a first. Moving quickly but carefully has paid off in multiple instances.

Before moving back to BPM, we want to make two points about the substantial risks of not collecting and analyzing data first. This shortfall is more common than it should be and is most likely to occur when analysts too firmly believe they already know the answer to the KIQ.

First, credibility can be lost. Consumers often read the text first and then look for additional data in the accompanying table or chart that reinforces or adds detail to the message, especially if it is quantitative. Consumers frequently home in on the numbers and may well do their own math. If the results are not inconsistent with the text, one of two things will happen: the piece will be tossed, or they make a phone call to your managers because they believe the data is cherry-picked to support an agenda. Neither is a good outcome.

Second, the consumer becomes the analyst. When the data and data analysis are not clear, consumers will try to develop their own net assessment of what they are supposed to take away from the piece. When consumers develop their own conclusions, analysts become bystanders with no control over the message.

EXAMPLE: Back to BPM

Develop a Collection Plan that Answers the Consumer's KIQ

Below is a model of how the Task Force was able to draw on consumer knowledge and the well-crafted KIQ to collect only the data needed to answer the question in-depth. Note that the collection was targeted and then arrayed in a table that allowed them to assess what the data said to answer the question. More on this below. As a reminder, here is the refined question: To what extent is BPM positioned to expand into Southeast Asia in a way that can protect the company's intellectual property?

Below is a list of some of the Sub-questions that the Task Force has or plans to answer. Recall that the group will select only the most essential Sub-questions at this point and put them in order to help structure their assessment.

1) Key potential Sub-questions that the Task Force must research to answer the KIQ include:

- How would we characterize the reliability of the potential partner?
- What alternatives might exist to locating a plant in Southeast Asia?
- How would an outside expert assess our insider threat program?

- What environmental laws would impact the manufacturing facility's location?
- How extensive is the regional market for our product?
- What is the record of the legal system in defending foreign investors?
- What is the record of the legal system's enforcement?
- What is the level of the cyber threat and record of local computer intrusions?
- Are there sufficient local workers and managers qualified to staff the plant?
- What is the potential to relocate managers from our plant here to Southeast Asia?
- What restrictions exist on profit repatriation?

2) Beyond already consulted sources, what other data might the task force want to collect?

- Information from on-site visits in Southeast Asia to fill gaps in the company's understanding of the potential risks.
- Views of US-based companies there and local US Chamber of Commerce there.
- Insights from the US Embassy and local US-based legal firms.

EXERCISE: Develop a Data Collection Plan that Answers the Consumer's KIQ

Instructions:

Turn to Chapter 4 in your Workbook.

The below chart is an example illustrating BPM's use of the Data collection framework.

Data Collection Framework		
Sub-Question	**Quantitative Data Source(s) Likely to be Relevant**	**Qualitative Data Source(s) Likely to be Relevant**
To what extent will a suitable manufacturing facility be available?	World Bank or national reports of size and number of industrial zones in Southeast Asian countries	Southeast Asia country reports from US Chamber of Commerce and manufacturing trade associations
To what extent can the local labor market provide sufficiently skilled staff and management personnel?	World Bank or national reports of median educational level in Southeast Asian countries	Southeast Asia country reports from US Chamber of Commerce and manufacturing trade associations

Figure 8. Example of BPM's Data Collection Framework

To get ready:

- Review your consumer's requirements.
- Make sure the KIQ is readily visible and recall what type of assessment is needed (context, explanation, trend assessment, warning, etc.).

Displaying the patterns in the data which you have collected in graphical form is an important step in your data analysis. In preparation for making your own graphic format selections, read the standards for data collection and visualization below.

ODNI Quality Standards Apply to Visuals

Data collection and visualization graphics are not ends in themselves. Rather, they are critical to helping you and your consumer spot changes in trends, patterns, and relationships in stories you know your consumer is following. And they will also help ensure that the analysis is derived from the data. For this reason, as early as 2015 the US intelligence services adhered to the rule that visuals and written intelligence assessments shared the same analytic standards for clarity and relevance.

Here is a summary of the ODNI graphics standards:

Visuals present one key point that jumps out at the viewer.

- Introductory language tells readers what they are seeing and ties it to the text.
- Visuals are placed near where their content is first discussed.
- Legends are easy to understand, color schemes are clear and understandable to color-blind decision makers.
- Date of information is clearly marked.

Visuals send a clear message because they:

- Help to answer the decision maker's KIQ
- Must be consistent with the text
- Add or clarify information (context, background, data)
- Highlight or expand on aspects of the B.L.U.F.

Visuals present compelling reasons for accepting the graphic's significance.

- Visuals are well sourced and explain information gaps.
- Visuals do not play on emotions.
- Avoid photos or language intended to generate sympathy.

See our observations in the Workbook on any quality issues related to the graphics.

EXERCISE: Decide on a Graphic Format that Will Help You Analyze the Data

Instructions:
Turn to Chapter 4 in the Workbook.

List specific ideas on how you will array the data which you will collect: maps, table, charts. Use the example below from the BPM scenario as your guide. Be patient. Review the data carefully. This step really matters because it will drive the rest of the exercises.

EXAMPLE: BPM's Graphic formats

BPM's Task Force visualizes charts for the quantitative data collected and tables for the qualitative data. For example.

Country	Median Years of Education	Estimated Availability of Skilled Workers
Indonesia	9	Medium
Malaysia	11	Medium
Philippines	10	Medium
Singapore	12	Medium
Thailand	9	Low

Figure 9. Availability of skilled local staff and management personnel in Southeast Asia

SUMMARY EXERCISE: Bridging from What's Known to What's Next

Turn to the end of Chapter 4 in the Workbook.

At this point analysts have identified their consumer, determined the KIQ, and gathered and analyzed the data required to answer it. From here on they begin the step-by-step process of assessing what the analyzed data tells consumers about What's Next. That data-driven response includes estimating the probability that they will reach their desired state or an event or development will occur, what it means for their organizations, and potential steps to improve the outcome.

Your answers to the questions below will pull together the hard thinking you have completed in the exercises so far and help you start to see the "connective tissue" that will shape your analytic product. So make sure you have filled in any gaps in the already completed frameworks.

Instructions:

You have already done the initial hard thinking. So use what you have done in your Workbook, but know that you will still make multiple changes along the way.

Answer the following questions in the Workbook drawn from the first four chapters.

- What is the new development that made you write? (Recent reporting indicates, suggests, or points to a new trend, pattern, or relationship)

- Who is the specific consumer for the product; who can/needs to act on the analysis?
- Why are you writing now? (This matters now because . . . .)
- What are your consumer's KIQ and sub-questions?
- What data did/will you collect to answer the question?
- How does it work? (Is there a process or terminology that needs to be explained, such as money laundering?)
- How do you plan to array the data?
- What is the impact so far? (The arrayed data indicates that so far the development has prompted . . . .)

CHAPTER FIVE

Draw Inferences from the Data

> "Data and data sets are not objective; they are creations of human design. We give numbers their voice, draw inferences from them, and define their meaning through our interpretations."
>
> —Kate Crawford, Harvard Business Review

GOAL: To understand how the structure of inferences (Fact A + Fact B implies → C) transitions analysts from What's Known to What's Next, expressed in data-driven response to the consumer's KIQ that marks the first estimate of the likelihood that they will reach their desired outcome or an event or development will occur.

Key Learning Objectives

At the end of this chapter, analysts will be better able to:

- Understand how *Intelligent Analysis* structures your analyzed data in the form of an inference (A + B → C) to answer the KIQ that includes an estimated probability that your consumer will reach their desired state.
- Make a (very tentative) first draft of an inference based on your own assessment using the structure A + B → C, which draws on the data collected and arrayed to answer your consumer's KIQ that includes the estimated probability. Subsequent chapters will help you refine the draft.

Note: As a refresher, go back to Chapter 1 and reread the section entitled: "Three Concepts Shape How We Look Ahead" and review the key terms. Recall especially the hierarchical relationship between the inference, assumptions, and data. This chapter includes multiple terms that may be unfamiliar, especially those around the most likely outcome and expressing levels of estimated probability. Do not be concerned. We will explain these concepts, and your product will be revised as you complete them in subsequent chapters. For now, just focus on the purpose of inferences and how they are formulated.

Inferences Link What's Known to What's Next

Nassim Taleb described inferences as the only way to "glimpse the future" (Taleb, 2010). The level of certainty expressed in Taleb's "glimpse" is at the heart of *Intelligent Analysis*. Specifically, how close does that "glimpse" come to being considered a fact. Viewed within the framework of our hierarchy (A + B →C), reaching that level of certainty almost certainly is based on the quality and reliability of the data collected and analyzed in the previous chapter, and we will address using SATs again in Chapter 8. Put simply:

- The inference moves closer to being a fact as high-quality data from good sources strengthen the validity of the assumptions that must hold in order to support the estimated level of probability of What's Next (likely, highly likely) based on Facts A + B.

- The inference moves away from being a fact as lower-quality data from questionable sources reduces the validity of the assumptions that must hold in order to support the estimated level of probability of what's next (*likely, unlikely, about even*) based on Facts A + B. The inference may still hold but with a lower estimated probability.

Underscoring the importance of inferences, the US intelligence services are required to start every written assessment and oral presentation with an inference that directly answers their consumer's KIQ.

Definitions Abound: Yet Again More Reinforcement

Inferences have multiple definitions. Below is the construct we use to help you craft an inference that answers the KIQ developed for your product.

A (fact as known) + **B** (fact as known) → **C** (the inference/conclusion)
"what" + "what" implies "so what"

- A and B are the facts as known at the time that they emerge, ahead of drafting, from the tables, charts, or maps you created in Chapter 4 to answer the consumer's KIQ.

- The arrow (→) is a recognized symbol for implies. For our purposes, implies means how closely do facts A + B support the assumptions that imply that C is an absolute fact based on data currently available.

- Short of being an absolute fact, which is extremely rare in intelligence analysis, how close A + B implies an absolute fact is expressed with caveats along a scale (*highly likely, likely, unlikely*) of certainty. We offer much more on assessing the reliability and quality of data in Chapter 8.

Analysts' answers to their consumers' KIQs are always expressed as inferences using this same two-part structure (A + B → C) where part 1) is the "what," the facts (A + B) developed during your targeted data collection, and part 2) is the "so what," what you can infer from the facts.

Specifically, the "so what" is made up of the changes in the as-is state (recall Chapter 4) derived from your arrayed and analyzed data. Analyzing and reporting on changes in the as-is state are what analysts do every day. These changes are always expressed as increases or decreases (or status quo) in trends, patterns, or relationships among the facts that change the as-is state and impact—or not—your consumer's priority and long-term issues that you and your consumer agreed on in Chapter 3.

(ICD, 203; Taleb 2008a; Taleb 2008b)

Differing Assumptions About the Same Data that Shape Inferences and Divide Us

First, consider two hypothetical commuters.

Driver 1: The Optimist.

1. Inference: Conclusions drawn from known facts. The formulation looks like this:

A (fact as known)	+	B (fact as known)	→	C (conclusion)
Clear roads	+	good weather	implies	I will be home in an hour.

2. Assumptions: Our driver assumes based on what is known at the time of departure that the roads and weather will remain clear and that no other conditions exist that could slow them down, such as the car remains functioning, gas supply is sufficient, and accidents are avoided. They are feeling lucky.

3. Data: Data is just data until it is arrayed and analyzed. Our driver has already sorted that out by looking online and listening to the radio. If that analyzed collected data remains unchanged, the estimated probability of an easy commute will remain an absolute fact. If new information comes in—traffic is backed up or the check engine light comes on—another caveat will have to be chosen based on what the new data indicate. The driver will get home but the likelihood of arriving on time diminishes to "probably" or worse.

Driver 2: More Cautious.

Another driver, however, looks at the same data and (however unlikely) makes the same assumptions at the time of departure but is less certain that those assumptions will hold and so concludes that their driving time will probably be sixty minutes. This driver starts out on much firmer analytic ground, but is also subject to change with the analysis of new information. Driving time could improve or worsen, requiring a new assessment of the estimated drive time.

BPM Task Force Drafts Their Lead Inference

The Task Force reviewed their analyzed data and developed an agreed-upon initial assessment of what emerged.

- (Fact A as known): Reliable data documents inconsistent legal protections for intellectual property in Southeast Asia

  +

- (Fact B (as known): A high-risk cyber threat environment

  Implies →

- (C): That although BPM can open a plant there our software is highly vulnerable to insider threats.

Assume, however unlikely, that the Board of Directors looks at the same data and the same operating environment but assumes it can be managed, a view reflected in their inference.

- Fact A (as known): Our review of Brighton Steel's insider threat program

  +

- Fact B (as known): Its record of successfully detecting and thwarting multiple threats against our intellectual property

  Implies →

- (C): That working with a local partner, BPM is highly likely to manage the risks associated with opening and operating a plant in Asia.

We will see how these sharp differences become the focus of the Task Force's work as they prepare their assessment for their senior managers.

Be Careful Drawing Inferences from Inferences

Making a follow-on inference from an implied relationship between facts raises risks of generating misleading conclusions. The construct of an inference drawn from an inference would look like this: A + B → C → D. This formulation tells your audience that the implied relationship between the facts and C can be the basis for inferring D, even if it is at a different level of probability. But is inferring D always a risk? The answer is, of course, it depends. D is an inference drawn from an inference, that can either enhance the inference or mislead consumers. Let's turn back to the commuters to illustrate the impact of drawing an inference from an inference.

Example:

Fact A (fact as known: reports of clear road +

Fact B (fact as known): good weather

→ implies

C: I will be home in an hour

D: and enjoy dinner with the family

(Again, D still depends on Facts A and B holding up.)

Implies →

E: I can expect the same travel time tomorrow

The point here is that the further analysts move away from the data the more they are just guessing because there are no data to support it.

EXERCISE: Draft a Lead Inference that Summarizes Your Message

Instructions:

Turn to Chapter 5 in the Workbook.

Draft an inference that captures your product's message using the A + B → C formulation. Understand that this is just a first effort that will be refined as we move forward.

A: (fact as known)

+

B: (fact as known)

Implies → implies a relationship between the two facts (estimated level of probability), which leads the consumer to

C: inference drawn from facts A + B

CHAPTER SIX

Draft Your Bottom Line Up Front

> **"The most important sentence in any article is the first one. If it doesn't induce the reader to proceed to the second sentence, your article is dead."**
>
> —William Zinsser, *On Writing Well*

GOAL: To introduce the purpose and structure of the B.L.U.F., explain why the inference the analysts drafted must lead the first paragraph, and produce a draft B.L.U.F. It will be refined as we move through the remaining chapters.

Key Learning Objectives

At the end of this chapter, analysts will be better able to:

- Explain the importance of the B.L.U.F. in *Intelligent Analysis* and why it must lead the B.L.U.F. paragraph.
- Explain the flow of the B.L.U.F.'s eight elements and how they are connected.
- Prepare a first draft of the B.L.U.F. for your intelligence product.

Note: This exercise is a first draft. Although the book has so far covered only What's Known—the first four elements—we decided to place this chapter here to preview how the B.L.U.F elements will flow. BPM's model B.L.U.F. below includes the title (covered in this chapter), your drafted lead inference, plus all eight B.L.U.F. elements. Subsequent chapters will break down and explain each element. There will be ample opportunities to refine each for your product.

Constructing the B.L.U.F. is Methodical, Demanding Work

With this chapter we shift from What's Known to developing the most likely outcome—What's Next. In the first paragraph of any analytic product, a well-constructed B.L.U.F. answers the KIQ, conveying actionable intelligence in a fixed format. As mentioned before, it includes all eight of the required elements. Two additional upfront elements included ahead of these eight elements make the product's message accessible to busy readers:

- First, an analytic title developed following the drafting exercise captures the inference's message in no more than ten words (Cariens 2012; Major 2009).

- Second, the inference developed in Chapter 5 leads the paragraph. The eight elements follow, adding detail.

Looking ahead, Chapter 8 focuses on assessing the data's reliability and quality. That assessment follows the inference. The title, lead inference, and eight elements that for us make up the B.L.U.F. are the foundation of every written analytic product and oral presentation of any length. Their succinctness and consistency deliver actionable intelligence in a clear message that explains the "what" and the "so what" and the "so what of the so what" and why it matters, which are discussed in Chapter 10. These qualities, and how clearly and quickly the B.L.U.F. tells a complete story, are its most important strengths. The consumer comes to expect this same format and structure every time. Below is a review of the B.L.U.F.'s elements, each of which will be explored in detail and practiced in later chapters.

Once More, Review the B.L.U.F.'s flow:

1. **What?** What development or event has prompted the KIQ? This refers to the development, new data, or change that needs to be reported based on the consumers' near- and long- term requirements. For example, weather data over the last two weeks points to signs of a drought.

2. **Why now?** Why is it happening now? All changes that can answer this question are expressed as a new one of the following:

- **Trend:** the development reflects an increase or decrease; what does the data say?
- **Pattern:** the development reflects a shift in what had been predictable behavior.
- **Relationship:** the development establishes that an event or action was a direct cause that made another event happen. A change in X (cause) produces a change in Y (effect). Or think of it this way: the cause = why it happened and the effect = what happened.

3. **How does it work?** Is there a process or terminology to be explained? This element is included when the development is a process or flow that requires explanation of how it works. Here the BPM Task Force might include more in-depth data on insider threats.

4. **What's the impact so far?** What has happened because of the development or event? The impact explains the size, scope, and outcome to date. For example, the scope and range of insider threats continues to spread into new industries and small businesses with valuable intellectual property.

From the known . . . to the unknown:

5. **What's ahead?** What's the "so what" for the analyst's consumer?

- The most likely outcome, or the "so what," and other possible outcomes are based on what can be inferred (more, less, better, worse, no change) from what is known.
- It includes an estimated level of probability that the desired outcome will be reached or an event or development will occur, such as BPM's goal of safely opening a plant in Southeast Asia.

6. **What are the implications for the most likely outcome?** For consumers it is the "so what of the so what" that explains the importance of what's ahead—why should it matter to the consumer.

7. **What mitigation strategies would help manage the risks and/or exploit opportunities?** The goal here is to improve the likelihood of meeting the consumer's goal by addressing weaknesses or uncertainties in the conditions that most impact the outcome.

8. **What indicators can be developed to gauge the strategies' effectiveness?** Indicators are metric driven and tied to each strategy. They are transparent and readily accessible to consumers.

To Start, Break Old Habits: The B.L.U.F.'s Pyramid Points Up

The below graph shows two very different structures for whatever analysts are writing, but only one, the B.L.U.F., meets the requirement for how to answer the consumer's question. Placing the bottom line on the bottom, or B.L.O.B., means a long journey to find the analyst's message. Rushed consumers are likely to become quickly frustrated and not bother hunting for your bottom line.

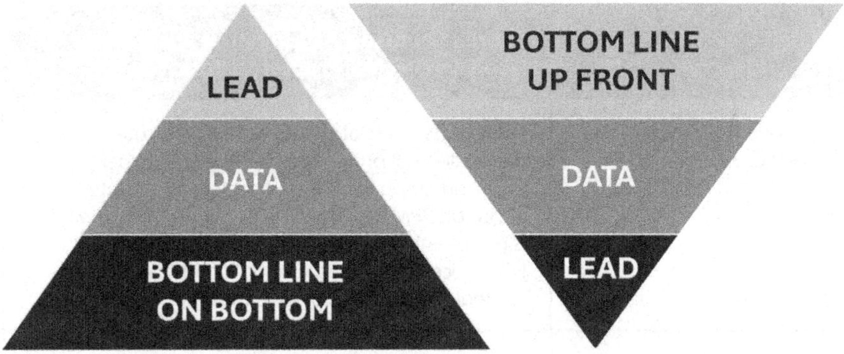

Figure 10. Intelligent Analysis bans the B.L.O.B. and embraces the B.L.U.F.

The B.L.O.B. is all about the writer; the B.L.U.F. is all about the consumer. Be the consumer's servant.

The model below picks up the work of BPM's Task Force with their first draft of an eventual response to the Board of Directors' assessment in the form of a B.L.U.F. Note how each element is structured and entered into the framework in one sentence and how the "connective tissue" creates a coherent response to the agreed-upon KIQ.

EXAMPLE: Task Force's Draft Response to Board of Directors' KIQ

Figure 9 below is the BPM Task Force's draft review of the Board of Directors' optimistic assessment. Clearly, it is overly long but is meant to underscore that the title and lead inference must convey the full answer to the KIQ and stand alone as a component of the detail in the subsequent eight elements. The Task Force will review and refine each element as we move through the steps. Then add the title and move to the last four B.L.U.F. elements.

Recall the approved KIQ followed by the Task Force's draft response:

- To what extent is BPM positioned to expand into Southeast Asia in a way that can protect the company's intellectual property?

Title	Board's Southeast Asia Initiative: Plant Looks Good, Intellectual Property at Risk
Inference that Captures the B.L.U.F.	Reliable data reveal inconsistent legal protections for intellectual property and a high-risk cyber threat environment in Southeast Asia, which indicates that although BPM can open a plant there our software is highly vulnerable to insider threats, and the Task Force recommends assessing potential mitigation strategies before deciding to move forward.
New Development ("what")	The Board of Directors wants to open a manufacturing facility in Southeast Asia and estimates the initiative is highly likely to succeed; the senior managers disagree.
Why Now?	The Board sees a growing market and their own analysis of Southeast Asia shows the company's proprietary software can be protected against insider threats.
How Does It Work?	The Board of Directors wants to use a local partner to help BPM navigate the bureaucracy and related challenges to opening the plant.
What is the Impact So Far?	No decision has been made, and the Board agreed with the senior managers to establish a Task Force to assess potential vulnerabilities.
What's Next? ("so what")	The Task Force reported to the senior managers that, while the plant can certainly be built, the company's software would be highly vulnerable to insider threats.
What are the Implications for the Consumer ("so what of the so what")?	The managers agreed and convinced the Board to step back, but the Board wanted an assessment of potential mitigation strategies that would help them meet their goal.
Potential Mitigation Steps and Indicators of Strategies' Effectiveness	Examples in Chapter 10. The focus is on the mitigating strategies for the two Linchpin assumptions.

Figure 11. Analysts' draft B.L.U.F. starts the structured discussions

EXERCISE: Build the B.L.U.F. for Your Product

Instructions:
Turn to Chapter 6 in the Workbook.

- Use the blank framework.
- Make sure that the first four elements you have worked on are complete, clearly written, and entered into the summary template at the end of Chapter 5.
- Follow the Task Force's model and review the explanations of each element earlier in the chapter.
- Fill in each element with a full sentence.

As each step is completed, look for the linkages—the connective tissue—between each element that delivers a strong lead paragraph and answers the consumers' KIQ.

One Last Step: Analytic Titles are Contracts with Consumer

Titles matter.

Note the language in the B.L.U.F. It is aligned with both the lead inference and the B.L.U.F. elements. They are the entry point for busy consumers that will likely decide—in seconds, yes, seconds—whether to read on, even if it does answer their KIQ. Write analytic titles, not descriptive ones. In fact, a strong title—combined with a strong lead inference, the B.L.U.F., and good graphics that reinforce the message—make for a powerful and consistent product.

The list of unhelpful, if catchy, titles in magazines, journals, and yes, even newspapers, is almost endless. *The Economist*, for example, prides itself on clever titles in the form of puns that rarely capture the story line. The same is true for the overly catchy subtitles. *Intelligent Analysis* does not do catchy. Do not use them, ever.

Good title standards do the following:

- Alert the consumer at a glance about a story
- Answer the consumer's question
- Capture B.L.U.F. elements, including the judgment's level of certainty, in eight to eleven words

- Avoid sensationalism or hype that can mislead readers
- Avoid the distractions and lack of clarity that come from puns and attempts at humor

The two titles below are examples from *The Economist* that fall short of these criteria. They are lifted from the March 16, 2019, issue, but *The Economist's* penchant for puns as titles remains unchanged. We offer the following (less humorous) alternatives that convey a simpler, clearer message:

- "The Aircraft Industry, Plane Truths: The crash of Ethiopian airlines ET302 shows why a golden age for the world's aircraft may be over" (23 words)
    - Our revision: "The Aircraft Industry: ET302 Crash May Weaken Boeing, Airbus Monopolies" (10 words)
- "Mental Health, Shrinks, Expanded, There Are Not Enough Psychiatrists. Trained laypeople can often help" (14 words)
    - Our revision: Mental Health: Solving Psychiatrist Shortage May Include Trained Lay People" (10 words)

Below is an example of how a descriptive title can morph into one that is analytic and conveys the B.L.U.F.'s message:

1. *Guide to Insider Threats*, 2022 (descriptive)
2. *Guide to Insider Threats, How to Protect Your Insurance Company* (reportorial)
3. *Special Training Raises Awareness and Reduces Insider Threat Risk* (combines quantitative and qualitative data to tell the story)

EXERCISE: Craft a Title

For example, BPM's draft title, "Board's Southeast Asia Initiative: Plant Looks Good, Intellectual Property at Risk," is short and captures the message of the lead inference and the message more broadly. It is all the consumer needs to decide whether to read on.

See Chapter 6 in the Workbook.

Instructions:

Use BPM's draft title as a model. Based on your draft B.L.U.F., craft a title that meets the criteria (8–11 words) and aligns with the lead inference and meets the criteria. Then add it to the draft paragraph; again review and refine as needed.

EXERCISE: Convert Framework into a Standalone Paragraph

Recast the title, inference, and eight elements as a stand-alone paragraph outside the framework (copy and paste works). It will help you see the connective tissue between the B.L.U.F. and the KIQ more clearly.

CHAPTER SEVEN

Identify Key, Working, and Potential Linchpin Assumptions

> **"Probability is the measure of the likelihood that an event will occur."**
>
> **"Probability is not about the odds, but about the belief in the existence of an alternative outcome, cause, or motive."**
>
> —Nassim Taleb, *Fooled by Randomness*

GOAL: To gain a more complete understanding of how the certainty of each assumption—how close it is to a fact—determines how the estimated level of probability is caveated, and how the potentially serious impact of a poor understanding of assumptions diminishes the credibility of estimates of probability and raises serious risks for analysts and consumers.

Key Learning Objectives

At the end of this chapter, analysts will be better able to:

- Use SATs to distinguish between Working, Key, and Linchpin assumptions and select them for your analytic product.
- Explain the central role that clearly articulated assumptions play in estimating probability and the challenges of developing the most likely outcome.
- Avoid common mistakes in managing assumptions that raise the risks of misleading consumers.
- Develop Working and Key Assumptions for your project.

Assumptions Underpin Probability Estimates

Intelligent Analysis, through the lens of BPM, will show how the Task Force starts to use SATs to develop a report for the senior managers to present to the Board of Directors. It will assess the validity of the Board's choice of *highly likely* to characterize the likelihood that BPM can find a partner to open a plant in Southeast Asia that will protect the company's intellectual property against insider threats. The sequence requires the Task Force to first identify underlying assumptions—conditions that must persist to support the Board's estimated level of probability.

Yet Again, Another Reminder

Keep in mind that we are focusing on the choice of highly likely. It may well be that in fact a secure plant can be built, but the probability of protecting the software is much lower.

- **Inference:** Structured as (A + B → C) where C is the inference based on facts (A + B) as known; includes an estimated level of probability (e.g., *likely, unlikely*) that implies (→ C).
- **Assumptions:** Conditions that must persist to support the implied (→ C) estimated level of probability.
- **Data:** Qualitative or quantitative information assessed for quality that becomes the basis for facts (A + B).

To Set the Stage: A Story of How Two Travelers Estimate What Comes Next

Two people stand on one side of a bridge; we will call them Traveler 1 and Traveler 2. Both, of course, are analysts. They are looking across the canyon deciding whether to cross into uncertainty. All they know is what they have learned from their trip so far: the roads were consistently good and safe and the locals friendly and helpful. In fact, those on the other side of the canyon had told the locals they would be well received. They gave the travelers a guidebook and map that said the same. Still, given the risk involved the travelers decided to assess the probability that their trip would continue unhindered once they crossed the bridge. Being analysts, they started with a refined KIQ: To what extent do conditions on the other side of the bridge mirror conditions along the walk so far?

Next, they developed a short list of assumptions and conditions that had to persist to make the journey safe. Later in the chapter we detail how this list was compiled. Here is the list, in no particular order:

- Locals have direct, accurate knowledge about current conditions across the canyon.
- Locals on this side mean them well.

- The old map and guidebook are still accurate.
- The two will remain traveling companions.
- There is a safe way to return home from the other side.

The travelers reviewed the available data and separately assessed how well the available data supported each assumption—how close did the data come to making each assumption a fact. For example, at this juncture the last assumption is not close to being a fact—it is completely unknown but important. The travelers would need considerably more reliable data to even start testing that assumption.

Based on their review they answered their KIQ in the form of inferences (A + B → C):

- Traveler 1: Based on what is known so far, the path has been safe, and the locals have been reliably helpful, so we are likely to find a similar reception on the other side.
- Traveler 2: Based on what is known so far, the path has been safe, and the locals have been reliably helpful, so the chances are only about even that we will find a similar reception on the other side.

What's happening here? At bottom, the differences between them reflected how each assessed how well the same data supported their assumptions; that is, what could be inferred from data available at the time they were deciding what's next and subject to change with new information. Traveler 1 reviewed what was known and determined that the facts indicated that the required conditions were *likely* to persist. They would be fine crossing over.

Traveler 2 did not agree. The information was too limited and multiple questions remained unanswered, so the likelihood that the required conditions would persist was *about even*. The traveler said more data was needed to validate the assumptions.

These dynamics are readily apparent in the production of virtually all analytic products. The focus is on the assumptions even if the analysts do not understand that the assumptions they hold—consciously or not—are driving their assessment. The higher the quality and reliability of the data the more each assumption—the condition that must persist—moves toward being a fact, and the stronger the caveat which can be used to imply the relationship between what is known and what can be inferred from what is known.

And so it is with BPM. In this case the Board of Directors reviewed the data around the operating environment in Southeast Asia and is convinced that the data (A + B) supports the implication that it is *highly likely* that the conditions required to support their high level of probability exist now and will persist, in contrast to the Task Force's draft response to the senior managers, their consumer. Same data, different assumptions, different assessment. That happens all the time, consciously or not. It is the source of endless argument.

Developing Most Likely Outcome Carries Risks: Trust the Process

As analysts, keep in mind that your job is to provide an objective response to a known consumer's approved KIQ that includes the estimated probability—the likelihood—that they will reach their desired state or an event or development will occur. Our approach mirrors the process the US intelligence services have long used to validate the estimated level of probability of their most likely outcome.

However, for them and for you as analysts, providing that balanced, data-driven look-ahead remains the most challenging stage of *Intelligent Analysis*, because of the stakes involved and consumers' demands to help them identify and manage risks. Consciously or not, when consumers, especially those unfamiliar with *Intelligent Analysis*, pressure analysts for a look-ahead, they are really asking how closely the data supporting the assumptions come to making the implied inference a fact (will). Essentially, they are asking for a prediction rather than an estimated probability.

Think of it this way. In developing actionable intelligence each caveat (*likely, probably, highly likely/unlikely*) signals a different sense of assurance to the consumer (A + B → C) about how likely they will reach their desired outcome or an event or development will occur. More often than you might think, however, consumers do not agree with probability estimates that do not give them their "right" answer. They regard "estimates" as resulting from analysts just looking for cover if they are wrong. In these instances, think of *Intelligent Analysis* as a protective shield that will help analysts navigate difficult situations because their assessment is transparent, defensible, and repeatable.

Some challenges will be friendly, but most will not. Be prepared for probing or hypothetical questions that require an opinion that goes beyond the data.

Regardless, consumers will very likely push for more certainty than can be resolved even with a careful walk through the data. Especially if unfamiliar with your world, they may harbor unrealistic expectations about *Intelligent Analysis* and assume that analysts are equipped to literally predict the future, which of course we are not and do not.

In these situations, consumers are not asking innocent questions; they want to find a way to pull you away from the data to push the assessment more in their direction, to drag you beyond the data.

If they sense an opening, they can play to an analyst's desire to be supportive or to display their expertise. If analysts take the bait they may feel helpful, but in reality the back and forth invariably leads to more speculation and drifting further from the data. Unwary analysts will take the fall for a "bad call." Getting it right without being rooted in the data is just luck.

One more time: the further you drift from the data, the more risk of missteps. What is opined can quickly morph into reportable fact.

A Facilitator Joins the Task Force

To keep its work on track the BPM Task Force decided to bring in a facilitator who, of course, follows our approach.

To start, let's return to BPM's Task Force that is now going through the same process as our two travelers. To put this activity in perspective, based on the Board's statement the Task Force will be developing assumptions that they agree must hold for the Board's optimistic assessment to remain at their level of certainty (*highly likely*) that BPM can safely open a plant in Southeast Asia which will protect the company's G-Codes.

As another reminder, here is the inference that captures the Board of Directors' message to senior managers.

- "Based on our review of BPM's insider threat program and its record of successfully detecting and thwarting multiple threats against our intellectual property, the Board of Directors assesses that BPM is *highly likely* to manage the risk associated with opening and operating a plant in Asia, although it will require a careful review of the operating environment before moving forward."

Facilitators in SAT Discussions Manage Process, Protect Equities

Facilitators should be neutral and familiar enough with SATs to manage the process. Their participation helps the group stay focused on data rather than personalities and makes sure all voices are heard. Facilitators can also manage disruptors (see Chapter 10). The US intelligence services have used facilitators for years to good effect.

Task Force Starts Clarifying Assumptions

To start the assumption selection process, the facilitator reviewed and approved the Task Force's work so far and turned to the next step, developing Working and Key Assumptions. The real value of this exercise is in the structured discussion among all relevant stakeholders that is intended to minimize the impact of biases and emotions and keep the process focused on the data. While the process is best done with relevant stakeholders, if necessary it can also be accomplished on your own or with one partner. (Process drawn from Davis 1997; Heuer 1999; Taleb 2008a; Taleb 2008b)

Example: BPM Develops Working and Key Assumptions

Below are the results of the Task Force's assumptions exercise.

First, Develop Working Assumptions

To develop Working Assumptions, the Task Force listed as many of the most plausible conditions they could think of that must persist to support the estimated probability that the Board of Directors' initiative will be successful. There is really no limit to the number, but we have found that the typical group or individual can raise around twenty credible Working Assumptions before suggestions become more speculative. Note how they are all phrased in positive language (more on that later). Here is their list, all plausible:

- A manufacturing facility is available in a location with sufficient power.
- Raw materials are locally available.
- The plant can turn a profit within two years.

- Finished products can be easily exported back to the US.
- The potential partner's reputation for honesty and performance checks out.
- Our computer systems are sufficient to thwart insider threats.
- Machinery can be easily imported.
- Our software can be safely stored on hard discs.
- Profits can be repatriated easily.
- Intellectual property laws sufficiently protect proprietary processes.
- The local labor force is skilled or trainable.
- The local labor force can be vetted.
- There is a supportive community of US-based businesses in the region.
- The market for BPM's products will continue to expand.
- Courts enforce intellectual property violations.
- If needed, managers and supervisors from the US plant will be willing to transfer.

Second, Determine Key Assumptions

From the list of Working Assumptions, the Task Force must select no more than five or six Key Assumptions. These assumptions are deemed the most important to support the inference's estimated level of probability (*highly likely*). The limited number reflects what analysts agree are the maximum number of variables that can be managed to protect the estimated probability. We will see later why going much beyond that number may well require a change in the estimated probability.

After considerable discussion the Task Force decided that the following assumptions are the most important, the Key Assumptions:

- The potential partner's reputation for honesty and integrity checks out.
- Our computer security systems are sufficient to thwart insider threats.
- The local labor force can be vetted.
- The market for BPM's products will continue to expand.
- National intellectual property laws sufficiently protect proprietary processes.
- Courts enforce intellectual property violations.

Third, Determine the Linchpin Assumptions

These are the one or two assumptions that the Task Force will determine are the most critical strengths or vulnerabilities that will impact the consumer's likelihood of reaching the desired outcome or that an event or development will occur.

While mentioned here, the Linchpins are determined only after the Key Assumptions Check exercise in Chapter 9 is completed. For the purposes of illustration and for use in an exercise in Chapter 8, however, we have selected two assumptions from BPM's list of Key Assumptions as "stand-in" Linchpins:

- Potential partner's reputation for honesty and integrity checks out.
- Courts enforce intellectual property violations.

We will ask you to do the same as well in the assumptions exercise at the end of this chapter. We come back to replace your stand-in draft Linchpin Assumptions in Chapter 10 after you have completed the Key Assumptions Check for your project.

Agreed-Upon Caveats Create a Continuum of Estimated Probability

To tie the strength of an assumption—how close it is to a fact—to the estimated probability more consistently, analysts in the US intelligence services have used a standard set of agreed-upon terms intended to signal to the consumer the likelihood that they will reach their desired state or an event or development will occur (Office Director of National Intelligence ICD, 2015, 2016). Before the adoption of this standard, the meanings of caveats such as *probably, highly likely, and highly unlikely* were subjective and varied widely among and within the US intelligence services and were the source of endless arguments.

While the mandated common terminology has not fully resolved these differences or prevented some heated discussions among analysts, it has provided them and consumers with a sense of scale. There are two approaches. Figures 12 and 13 map caveats on two different continuums. Figure 14 is a table that includes additional caveats which analysts have used for decades to characterize the estimated probability of inferences.

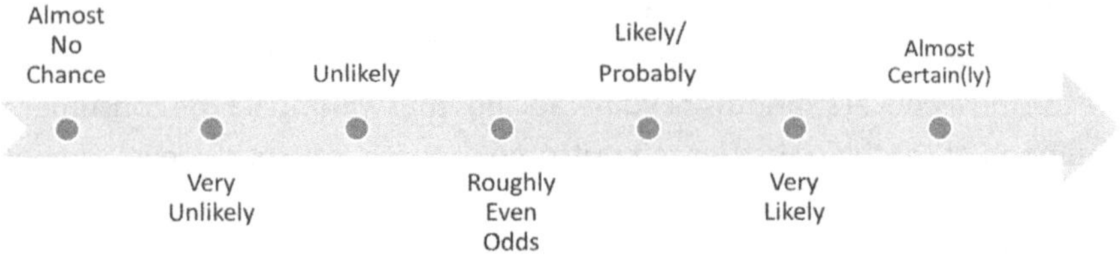

Figure 12. The continuum of Office Director of National Intelligence's vocabulary of probability.

Almost No Chance	Very Unlikely	Unlikely	Roughly Even Odds	Likely	Very Likley	Almost Certainly
Remote	Highly Improba-ble	Improba-ble	Roughly Even Odds	Probable	Highly Probable	Nearly Certain
1-5 %	5-20 %	20-45 %	45-55 %	55-80 %	80-95 %	95-99 %

Figure 13. Aligns caveats with likelihood expressed as percentages (source: Intelligence Community Directives [ICD], 203).

The chart below sets out the agreed-upon terms used to caveat inferences—to express how close an assumption is to being a fact (ICD, 203; 2015).

Office of Director of National Intelligence's Caveats Tied to Specific Percentages

- Remote
- Very Unlikely
- Unlikely/Even Chance
- Probably/Likely
- Very Likely
- Almost Certainly

In Descending Order: Other Caveats Analysts Use to Convey Decreasing Degrees of Probability

- Underscores
- Indicates
- Points to
- Suggests

Caveats That Express Conditional Probability

- Might
- Would
- Could
- Maybe/May
- Can

Meaningless Caveats

- A chance
- Cannot dismiss
- It's conceivable
- Perhaps
- In my view/opinion
- We believe/In our judgment (which express collective assessments of probability)

Figure 14. These caveats replace the arrow (→) symbol in the inference construct A + B → C.

Setting aside the ODNI's caveats in the upper left, here is an explanation of the other three quadrants, with examples.

- Caveats in the upper right quadrant are among the list of modal auxiliary verbs that express conditionality. Each has a specific meaning relative to expressing the probability of other less likely outcomes. In *Intelligent Analysis,* however, these caveats must be followed by "because," which signals an explanation of conditions that would move the possible outcome closer to being a fact.
  - **Example (correct use of conditional):** The new subway routes should quickly force cab drivers off the roads because of reduced long-haul fares into the city that make up over half their revenue.
  - **Example (incorrect use of conditional):** The new subway routes should quickly force cab drivers off the roads. (No reason is given.)
- Caveats in the lower left quadrant also signal the level of probability. They appear arbitrary but their significance is understood and used extensively among the US intelligence services. The terms are listed in relative order of certainty, ranging from the more tentative term *suggests* to *underscores* or *indicates*, which express more certainty.
  - **Example:** Over the last six months, park attendance has increased significantly, and multiple reliable sources report a 20 percent increase in climbing-related accidents during the same period, which *suggests/indicates/underscores* that inexperience is behind the spike in climbing-related accidents in the park.
  - Which caveat is used depends on the strength of the quantitative and qualitative data, including perhaps medical records and interviews with injured individuals and witnesses.

Terms listed in the lower right quadrant (murky and unhelpful) are banned from *Intelligent Analysis*. They are weak and misleading substitutes for a clear judgment and are often used to obscure a lack of data and to convince readers that expertise or an opinion alone is enough of a reason to support an assessment, which of course is not true. In fact, they are just guessing or predicting.

Reminder: Assumptions Are a Minefield—Avoid Traps

Testing assumptions is at the heart of estimating probability and of *Intelligent Analysis*. The central role of assumptions, however, also means that they pose the greatest risk to the accuracy of the B.L.U.F.'s lead inference, and, therefore, of the analyst's judgment. In fact, most arguments among analysts and with consumers center around estimating probability. Unconsciously or (less likely) consciously, a diverse group that starts out with the same data, like our two hikers, for example, almost always come to the table with their own perspective shaped by biases and experiences. And these differences are a good thing, but only if managed.

These differences show up most sharply in debate over which assumptions are the Key and Linchpin Assumptions and then over the reliability and quality of the data sources that support each assumption. Often, when participants have not or are unable to state their assumptions, strongly held—indeed, unmovable—views can surface that easily morph into personal arguments, and data is pushed to the sidelines and the process gets stuck.

These four rules, some of which have already been introduced, can help analysts avoid the most serious potential pitfalls.

Rule 1: Be sure assumptions are clearly stated in full sentences.

- Clearly articulating assumptions in writing forces analysts to think through the reasoning behind an estimated probability. It also makes an analyst's reasoning more transparent to the consumer and keeps the focus on the data, not personalities. In addition, it has become more common among the US intelligence services to state assumptions in even short assessments if there are wide differences among stakeholders. Some experienced senior consumers will ask for assumptions so they can better understand the arguments.

Rule 2: State assumptions positively.

As we have already made clear, assumptions are conditions that must exist, not conditions that must not exist, which could number in the dozens.

Examples:

- The courts are not biased (incorrect) vs. The courts remain unbiased (correct).

or

- The unions do not strike (incorrect) vs. Labor unions avoid strikes (correct).

Rule 3: Limit Key Assumptions to no more than five or six.

This point about limiting the numbers was raised earlier in the chapter, but it is worth repeating. Starting out with an extensive list of Working Assumptions is important because it allows analysts to think broadly about which assumptions are most important in supporting the estimated probability (*highly likely*) that supports the Board of Directors' assessment. This winnowing process is critical because, with any more than six conditions, there is less control over the outcome. To be clear, it is not that the other assumptions are unimportant, but that in the analyst's view they are not as essential in supporting the estimated probability.

Below is an example of what happens when the list of Key Assumptions goes beyond six. Let's use this inference to work with: Supply lines are secure, and labor relations and global demand are steady, so the company will likely meet this year's 10 percent growth target. This forecast is based on Key Assumptions:

- Shipping lanes remain open.
- Trucks are available as needed.
- Banks continue to provide financing.
- Labor relations remain good.
- Company leadership remains intact.
- Global suppliers can fill orders on time.

Now add five more:

- Ports are well maintained.

- Key customers remain under contract.
- Potential rivals lack access to parts.
- Hiring keeps up with expansion plans.
- Regulatory environment remains business-friendly.

The Key Assumptions now expand to eleven. The company, however, cannot reliably assume that all or even half of the eleven conditions that must persist will persist because that is too many for any organization to control. By control we mean ensure that vulnerabilities can be mitigated (see Chapter 10).

As a result, the company's operating environment becomes more complex, and it faces risks it cannot manage. So the estimated probability that the company *likely will* hit its growth target diminishes. The additional five Key Assumptions may well matter, but the company needed to list only the five or six that matter most. This dynamic is what makes data-driven discussions and the role of the facilitator so important.

Rule 4: New information must be continually integrated into the analysis.

Assumptions can become "frozen" when analysts fail to modify their expressed level of probability in the face of new information. Estimating the probability that consumers will reach their desired outcome or an event or development will occur must be a fluid process. If an analyst resists change—and this happens more than it should for lots of reasons—they could consciously or unconsciously start to look for, or give credence to, only data that reinforce their position. Also, recall that we emphasized that the KIQ may change as well with the new data.

A Special Focus: Frozen Assumptions can be Deadly

One more time: Frozen assumptions pose serious risks to *Intelligent Analysis.*

A corollary to Rule 4: As new information arrives and is integrated into the text, check for any other references that might have been made to the former draft. There are no easy fixes.

Failure to change the estimated probability in the face of new data is as dangerous as formulating a KIQ that answers the question in the question. In disregarding new information, analysts run the risk of misleading the consumer, who may well make decisions assuming the assessment is accurate and consistent with current data. Consider the potential consequences of an analyst's stubbornness (Davis 1997).

Analysts who feel compelled to cling to an assumption in the face of new data should consider another line of work.

EXERCISE: Develop Working, Key Assumptions and Stand-In Linchpin Assumptions

Instructions:

Turn to Chapter 7 in the Workbook.

If possible, do the exercise with at least one partner.

- Develop at least twelve Working Assumptions. Make sure they are stated positively and easily understood.
- Identify five or six Key Assumptions. From the list of Working Assumptions these are the five or six that best support the level of probability expressed in your inference as to whether the desired state will be reached or the development or event expressed in your inference will occur.

EXERCISE: Identify Potential Linchpin Assumptions

These are the one or two assumptions (recall they are only draft selections until Chapter 9) deemed the most critical to sustaining the estimated level of probability expressed in the inference.

Instructions:

Review your Key Assumptions and select two potential Linchpin Assumptions to be used in exercises in Chapters 8 and 9, where you will complete the Key Assumptions Check (KAC) for your project. In Chapter 10 exercises will help you determine the Linchpin Assumptions for your project.

CHAPTER EIGHT

Gauge Data's Level of Certainty/Quality

> **"Reliable data . . . refers to data that can be a trusted basis for analysis and decision-making."**
>
> —Talend Solutions, LLC

GOAL: To demonstrate how two different SATs help analysts gauge the Level of Confidence (LOC) they can have that the quality and reliability of their analyzed data supports each Key Assumption that underpins the caveat (likely, probably…) used to express the estimated probability in the lead inference.

Key Learning Objectives

At the end of this chapter, analysts will be better able to:

- Understand how the two different measures of confidence in the data—how well they support the assumption and their reliability—add an important dimension to probability estimates.
- Explain how the Source Assessment Framework helps make gauging the LOC more deliberate.

LOC: Assesses How Well Data Supports Facts A + B

Gauging the reliability of the data that support facts A + B in the inference is a separate and important measure of how well the data support the level of probability expressed in the inference. Specifically, the data can strongly support (or not) the facts (A + B), but the reliability/quality of the sourcing matter as well.

In this chapter we again return to data and look at how the US intelligence services have long used measures called the LOC to answer the question: "How do we know what we know and how reliable is the data?" Specifically, the LOC comprises two measures:

- How well does the data support the inference's estimated probability?
- What is the level of confidence in the data; how reliable is the source?

Statements of the LOC are mandated in the 2004 Intelligence Reform and Prevention of Terrorism Act. They are required because post-911 leaders in the US intelligence services perceived that many analysts, consciously or not, sometimes lowered or raised their estimates of probability because they were unsure of the quality of the information underpinning their assumptions at the time of drafting. The consumer, of course, would be unaware of the hesitancy, raising the risk of seeing an incomplete and unbalanced assessment (ICD 203). Expressing the LOC is not always required but is used most often when the reliability of the data helps put the estimate of probability in context, especially when dealing with tough analytic questions.

To avoid confusion, the probability estimate and the LOC must be expressed in two sequential sentences.

- The first sentence states the inference that includes the estimated probability of what is inferred.
- The next sentence must be a separate statement expressing the LOC in the data used to determine the estimated probability at the time of drafting. Both are subject to change with new information.

The LOC: A Warning—It is Not an Opinion

The LOC in the data is measured against a set of recognized criteria for evaluating sources, such as we have listed below. It is not a measure of your own confidence in the available data, which could be shaped by 1) a false sense of confidence in your judgment, which happens more often than it should; and 2) the belief that you have dug deeply enough into the available data to warrant that confidence.

Analysts instead need to ask themselves: what am I missing and where else should I be looking to ensure that analysis remains consistent with the data? The potential for new information to surface is the reason why the LOC must be expressed in a separate second sentence in the B.L.U.F. that also makes clear the estimated probability based on data available at the time of drafting and must be changed with new data. We will see later that the KAC helps manage these risks.

Consider, for example, the following inference (exaggerated for effect):

"The used car in the showroom looks great and the dealer has shown us a list of all the work that was done on the car and the unblemished CARFAX report, so the vehicle is *highly likely* to be a good purchase."

The weight of the data—the dealer's word and the repair list and CARFAX report—all indicate that the data support the estimated probability (*highly likely*) of a purchase. The next question, however, needs to be a review of the data's reliability. The CARFAX report is certainly solid but can the same be said for either the dealer's reputation or the list of fixes? So, without an assessment of the data, if the buyers go ahead they have settled for the dealer's word, which often raises the risk that the car is not as advertised.

Three Levels of Confidence Explained with Examples

To help analysts gauge the data's LOC, the National Intelligence Council (NIC), which is part of the ODNI's staff, has created a scale that describes how the reliability and quality of the data flesh out their relationship to the judgment, or in our case the inference, that provides important context for consumers (ODNI, ICD 203). Figure 15 below illustrates the scale.

High Confidence	• The judgments are based on high-quality information, and/or the nature of the issue makes it possible to render a solid judgment. *But* • A "high confidence" judgment is not a fact, and there is still risk of being wrong.
Moderate Confidence	• The information is credibly sourced and plausible, but not of sufficient quality or corroborated sufficiently to warrant a higher level of confidence
Low Confidence	• The information's credibility and/or plausibility is questionable. • The information is too fragmented or poorly corroborated to make solid inferences. • We have significant concerns or problems with the sources.

Figure 15. LOC established by the ODNI add transparency and context for consumers.

Returning to the decision to purchase the car, here's an example that shows how both measures would work in sequence.

> The used car in the showroom looks great and the dealer has shown us a list of all the work that was done on the car and the CARFAX report, so the vehicle is *highly likely* to be a good purchase. I have only *moderate confidence* in this assessment, however, because my decision relies in large part on the reputation of the dealership which needs further examination.

To be clear, the estimated probability (*highly likely*) was justified based on data available at the time of the showroom visit, but the question of the reliability of the data about the list of work completed rests on the dealer's record that requires additional data to validate. If the additional reliability data shores up the inference, the LOC increases and the purchase becomes more likely.

The box below illustrates how the level of confidence looks in practice in a declassified Intelligence Community Assessment on global water security published in 2012 (ICA, "Water") that the ODNI opted to release (they are necessarily dated products). Note that in the first key judgment (A), the level of certainty is high, based on what is known, but there is only a moderate level of confidence in the sourcing because of the gaps in the information.

Water Security: Key Judgments Separate Probability from LOC

A. We assess that during the next ten years, water problems will contribute to instability in states important to US national security interests. Water shortages, poor water quality, and floods by themselves are unlikely to result in state failure. However, water problems—when combined with poverty, social tensions, environmental degradation, ineffectual leadership, and weak political institutions—contribute to social disruptions that can result in state failure.

We have moderate confidence in our judgment, as we have reliable open-source data on water pricing and infrastructure investments and reliable but incomplete all-source data on water quality.

B. We assess that a water-related state-on-state conflict is unlikely during the next ten years. Historically, water tensions have led to more water-sharing agreements than violent conflicts. However, we judge that, as water shortages become more acute beyond the next ten years, water in shared basins will increasingly be used as leverage; the use of water as a weapon or to further terrorist objectives also will become more likely beyond ten years.

We have high confidence in our judgments because there are excellent all-source reports on future water shortages and a well-established pattern of water problems aggravating regional tensions.

Note the clear separation of the estimated probability from the LOC.

The Source Assessment Framework Measures Reliability and Quality

To help make source assessments more deliberate we created an SAT that combines both measures in one framework. For the purposes of illustration, we are going to use one of the two potential draft Linchpin Assumptions we selected from the Task Force's list of Key Assumptions in Chapter 7. Recall, however, that in the flow of *Intelligent Analysis*, Linchpins will not be definitively selected until after the KAC is completed in the next chapter. Below is a short list of source evaluation criteria drawn from multiple sources:

- Expertise: What does the author know about the subject?
- Objectivity: Does the author have an agenda?
- Documentation: Where did the author get the information?
- Timeliness: When was the material written?
- Review and editing: Was the material peer-reviewed for publication?
- What is the reputation of the media where the source first appeared?

Two Measures Assign Numerical Ratings to Gauge Data Quality, Reliability

Figure 16 below introduces two measures that use numerical ratings (1–10). We rate the reliability and quality of the data supporting both measures that are then integrated into the Source Assessment Framework. For illustration purposes we use the Task Force's two draft Linchpin Assumptions selected in Chapter 7.

While we discuss each measure separately, we combine them in the Source Assessment Framework to illustrate how they work in tandem to develop the LOC. From their ratings the Task Force determines the overall source rating that becomes the basis for the B.L.U.F.'s second sentence in the lead paragraph.

Measure 1) *How well does the data support facts A + B?* Rate on a 1–10 scale (10 highest).

1–3: weak or conflicting data
4–6: generally good but limited
7–10: wide range of consistent supporting data

Measure 2) *What is your LOC in the data: how do we know what we know? Rate it on a scale of 1 to 10 (highest)?* A reminder of the ODNI's LOC ratings:

High Confidence (7-10)	• The judgments are based on high-quality information, and/or the nature of the issue makes it possible to render a solid judgment. *But* • A "high confidence" judgment is not a fact, and there is still risk of being wrong.
Moderate Confidence (4-6)	• The information is credibly sourced and plausible, but not of sufficient quality or corroborated sufficiently to warrant a higher level of confidence
Low Confidence (1-3)	• The information's credibility and/or plausibility is questionable. • The information is too fragmented or poorly corroborated to make solid inferences. • We have significant concerns or problems with the sources.

Figure 16 below shows BPM's completed evaluation of key sources.

EXAMPLE: BPM Task Force Evaluates Key Sources

1. B.L.U.F.'s Lead Inference	2. Name of Source)	3. How well do the data support facts A + B (certainty)	4. What is your LOC in the data? How do we know what we know?	5. Source Rating (& comment)
Enter the assumptions that must persist to support it.		7–10: Supporting 4–6: Good but limited 1–3: Weak, conflicting	7–10: High 4–6: moderate 1–3 Low	
Potential partner's reputation for honesty and integrity checks out.	Multiple interviews with local sources.	Rated: 4	Rated: 5 Confident but information is limited.	Rated: 4 Results were mixed; overall relationships were often superficial and unverifiable.
Courts enforce intellectual property violations.	Decision data from local appellate courts.	Rated: 7	Rated: 7	Rated: 7 Overall records were good, but more needed from local litigants.
Additional sources				

Figure 16: BPM's Source Assessment Framework looks at Linchpin Assumptions.

Below is the Task Force's lead inference followed by their LOC statement based on the two measures and the evaluation criteria:

> Reliable data document inconsistent legal protections for intellectual property, and a high-risk cyber threat environment in Southeast Asia indicates that although BPM can open a plant there our software is *highly likely* to be vulnerable to insider threats, and the Task Force recommends assessing potential mitigation strategies before deciding to move forward. We have only moderate confidence in our assessment because the data on the challenges and opportunities that come with deciding to move forward varies widely, but overall well-documented loopholes in the legal framework and a mixed re-

cord of court decisions raise concerns about transparency and BPM's ability to protect its interests.

Source Assessment is Critical to AI:

The literature related to artificial intelligence (AI) and machine learning (ML) underscores two key points we have made throughout this and our first book.

The validity of what can be inferred from the data depends on the assumptions that are made and the quality and reliability of the data that support them. And the assumptions and data must be continually retested. Models do not give you THE answer. They give you AN answer that must be tested. The *Intelligent Analysis* process should remain central to developing assessments every time.

EXERCISE: Complete the Source Assessment Framework

Instructions:

Turn to Chapter 8 in the Workbook.

- Recall for the purposes of illustration that you will use the two potential Linchpin Assumptions selected in Chapter 7.
- Using the two measures, source evaluation criteria, and rating guides, assess the most important sources for these two assumptions.

The blank template is below. Before going forward, however, first enter your draft lead inference in the Workbook so you can stay focused on assessing the sources that underpin the estimated probability.

1. B.L.U.F.'s Lead Inference	2. Name of Source)	3. How well do the data support facts A + B (certainty)	4. What is your LOC in the data? How do we know what we know?	5. Source Rating (& comment)
Enter the key assumption		Recall the rating guidance	Recall the rating guidance	
Enter the key assumption				
Overall ratings		Overall level of certainty	Overall level of confidence	Overall source rating

EXERCISE: Draft an Overall Source Rating Using Your Draft Linchpin Assumptions

Instructions:

In your Workbook

- For reference go back to Chapter 7 and copy the two draft Linchpin Assumptions selected from the list of Key Assumptions and enter them in the left column.
- Using the BPM example as model, complete the Source Assessment Framework.

Then complete the sentence below:

We have ___(high, medium, low) confidence in our estimated level of probability of the (assessment) because… (explain)

Source evaluation is a standard practice across multiple disciplines. It is a logical question which consumers are likely to raise as they review your assessment. Being prepared to respond with your completed frameworks will add important credibility and transparency to your assessment.

EXERCISE: Now Combine the Three Lead Elements of the B.L.U.F. Paragraph

Instructions:

Turn back to Chapter 6 in the Workbook where you completed a draft B.L.U.F.

- Based on completed exercises enter the following into the framework:
    - The title.
    - The lead inference.
    - The LOC statement as the second sentence.
    - Review for coherence; ensure your entries send a consistent message to your consumer.

CHAPTER NINE

Key Assumptions Check Tests Inference's Estimated Probability

> **"Rechecking assumptions can be valuable at any time prior to finalizing judgments, to ensure that the assessment does not rest on flawed premises."**
>
> —*US Government, A Tradecraft Primer: Structured Analytic Techniques for Improving Intelligence Analysis*

GOAL: To demonstrate how the KAC uses set criteria to rate the reliability and quality of data that supports the accuracy of What's Known (facts A + B), how those ratings in turn affect the validity of the other Key Assumptions, and the impact of each assumption on the estimated probability expressed in the caveated inference.

Key Learning Objectives

At the end of this chapter, analysts will be better able to:

- Understand the criteria used in the KAC to evaluate the impact of each assumption on the estimated level of probability (likely, unlikely…) expressed in an inference.
- For each assumption that must hold, validate the estimated probability expressed in your inference to complete the KAC framework based on the criteria across the top of the framework.
- Quantitatively assess the Key Assumptions underlying your inference's look ahead and the expressed estimated level of probability.

The KAC Tests the Inference's Estimated Probability

In *Intelligent Analysis*, the KAC is the most important SAT in the analyst's tool kit because of its direct impact on your thinking about What's Next and how to shape the answer to the consumer's KIQ. One way to think about it is to see the KAC as an X-ray of the KIQ's answer because the ratings tell a story about the validity of the inference and because it makes the analysis more transparent to your consumers, who can more readily see the reasoning and track the argument.

Specifically, the KAC framework brings together three separate but mutually reinforcing measurements that help analysts visualize how each assumption on its own and collectively aligns with the inference's expressed probability:

- How well the data supports the assumption

- The LOC in the sources
- The impact of each assumption on the ability of the others to persist if it does not hold up

(This chapter draws heavily on Tradecraft Primer, 2009; Davis 1997; Heuers 1999.)

Using the KAC matters most when the consumer's KIQ touches on a subject where there are significant differences among multiple stakeholders and data are either thin or overwhelming. The KAC has other important qualities. Most notably it:

- De-biases the analysis. Like the other tools integrated into *Intelligent Analysis*, it can help filter out emotions and biases and focus discussions on the data, not on personalities.
- Serves as both a quantitative and qualitative tool. That is, the numerical ratings used in the KAC to rate the inference's different dimensions are a result of structured, data-driven discussions that leverage expertise and diverse views, foster collaboration across different components, and help ensure that all voices are heard.
- Determines the Linchpin Assumptions.
- Tells a story. We will see in the next chapter how, when read across or down the table, the numbers further refine the inference that answers the consumer's question.

For these reasons, the US intelligence services label the KAC a "formal assumptions check" because the discussions are tightly structured and part of a facilitated process by a group that works with agreed-upon rules. The KAC can be used by a single analyst, but ensuring objectivity can be a challenge. It is best used with at least one collaborator, and the tool is even more effective when used to integrate competing views among multiple stakeholders.

The table below shows the blank KAC template. The scale for each column is 1–10. As you work through the KAC it is important to keep in mind that its sole purpose is to test the estimated probability (*likely, probably, unlikely, etc.…*) used to express the implied (→) relationship between the facts and the inference. BPM's completed KAC is in the next section. You will complete your own as an exercise. A guide to help determine the ratings is provided as we go through the methodology.

The Ratings Speak: Some Details

Let's start with the blank template and explanations of each column in Figure 17.

1. What assumptions must persist to maintain the validity of my most likely outcome? Write out each assumption that underpins the inference:	2. How strongly does the data support the inference's estimated probability? (1–10)	3. What is the level of confidence in the data? (1–10)	4. Would this assumption's failure cause any others to fail? (1–10)	5. What is the impact on the inference's estimated probability if the assumption doesn't hold? (1–10)
One too many				

Figure 17. The columns across and down tell a story.

What each column measures:

Moving left to right note how each column answers a different question to leave room to decide if the rating will weaken or strengthen the inference.

Column 1: List Key Assumptions. Initially, all have the same weight. Linchpin assumptions will emerge later from the completed framework. Remember to write the Key Assumptions in full to make sure they are clearly stated and understood.

Column 2: Based on a review of the data that support the level of probability, assign each assumption a strength-of-data rating. This rating answers the question: To what extent do the data currently available support the assumption?

Column 3: Drawing on lessons learned in the last chapter, assign an LOC rating to the source of the data for each assumption. This rating answers the question: To what extent are the sources reliable? Analysts gauge known biases or the quality of the quantitative and qualitative data, including polls and surveys.

Column 4: This column measures the assumptions' interdependence, which reflects the inference's complexity, that is, whether one assumption's failure to hold up may cause a cascading effect across the other assumptions. It answers the question: To what extent would this assumption's failure create a cascading effect?

Column 5: Rate the expected impact of each assumption on the inference's estimated probability. It answers the question: To what extent would this assumption's failure to hold force a change in the estimated level of probability of success?

> **Important Note:** This last rating is not a result of the averaging of the numbers in the previous columns, but a separate discussion of the impact on each assumption's impact on the estimated probability. Using an average would be deceptive because an assumption with high ratings in columns 2 and 3 and a low rating in column 4 could still have a high rating in column 5 even though its overall impact on the other assumptions is limited.

The Collective Story They Tell

Across each row the KAC evaluates the data that support each assumption and its impact on other assumptions that in turn test the caveat used to imply the relationship between What's Known and What's Next. Moving down the columns, the data provide a comparative perspective on the assumptions' validity (a more detailed guide follows).

Columns 2 and 3 assess how we know what we know (the LOC), and columns 4 and 5 assess the impact of the data's quality and reliability on the estimated level of probability. Think of it this way:

- An assumption supports the inference's estimated probability if the ratings are high (8–10) for columns 2 and 3, followed by low numbers (3–6) for columns 4 and 5. The message it sends is that reliable and high-quality data support the assumption, it has low impact on the other assumptions, and, at time of drafting, it has a measured impact on the assessment.
- An assumption is less supportive of the estimated probability if ratings in columns 2 and 3 are low (3–6), followed by high ratings in columns 4 and 5. The message here is that the supporting data are weak, and at the same time the failure of the assumption would have a cascading effect on the other assumptions, pointing to an important vulnerability that would likely require a lowering of the estimated probability, especially if selected as a Linchpin Assumption.

Figure 18 below is a guide we created for the KAC that provides language mapped to each numerical rating. The guide is in the Workbook as well and can be printed for reference. The Task Force's completed KAC with explanations of each column follows in the next section. Use the guide to help think through each rating.

KEY ASSUMPTIONS CHECK—RATING GUIDE

DATA CHECK: Columns 2 & 3				IMPACT CHECK: Columns 4 & 5	
	Level of certainty in data	**Level of confidence in source(s) of data**		**Cause other assumptions to fail**	**Impact on desired outcome**
0	There are no relevant data	There are no data, or the data source(s) have zero credibility	0	If this assumption fails, none of the other Key Assumptions will be affected	If this assumption fails, the desired outcome will not be materially affected
1			1		
2	There are negligible relevant data, and the data are incoherent	The objectivity and reliability of the data sources are highly questionable	2	If this assumption fails, it will marginally affect some of the other Key Assumptions	If this assumption fails, it will have a negative effect on the desired outcome

DATA CHECK: Columns 2 & 3				IMPACT CHECK: Columns 4 & 5	
3			3		
4	There are some relevant data, but the data are conflicting or incoherent	The objectivity and reliability of the data sources are questionable	4	If this assumption fails, several of the other Key Assumptions will be affected	If this assumption fails, it will have a significant negative effect on the desired outcome
5			5		
6	There is a significant amount of relevant data, but the data are not complete or consistent	The data sources are reasonably objective and reliable	6	If this assumption fails, several of the other Key Assumptions will be significantly affected	If this assumption fails, the desired outcome may or may not occur
7			7		
8	The relevant data are extensive, relatively complete, and consistent	The data sources have a strong track record of objectivity and reliability	8	If this assumption fails, several of the other Key Assumptions will fail	If this assumption fails, it is likely that the desired outcome will not occur
9			9		
10	The data are complete and consistent	The data sources are 100% objective and reliable	10	If this assumption fails, all of the other Key Assumptions will fail	If this assumption fails, it is almost certain that the desired outcome will not occur

Figure 18: Rating Guide provides context around each of the numbers on the scale.

Data-Driven Discussions Determine Task Force's KAC Ratings

Recall that at this point BPM's Task Force has developed a set of Key Assumptions which they assess are conditions that must persist to confirm the Board of Directors' estimated probability of success (highly likely) and that it can achieve the desired outcome—to safely establish the plant in Southeast Asia. The Task Force facilitator turns to the blank KAC template, ties it to the previously established Key Assumptions, and explains the meaning of each column and the ground rules for determining the ratings.

To be clear, the completed KAC and follow-up exercises do not capture the flow and often intense discussions around the ratings for each assumption (more on internal tensions in Chapter 10). With the facilitator's guidance, however, they generally stay focused on the data. When working as a group, reconciling diverse perceptions into a single rating in any of the columns can be time consuming, but it is the heart of the matter. Settling for compromises or accepting decision by consensus creates a lack of clarity for your consumer. Dissents surface, however (more on that later).

EXAMPLE: The Task Force's Completed KAC

Again, keeping the rating guide close will be helpful. Below in Figure 19 is the senior managers' approved KIQ, also Board supported, that the Task Force is answering:

- To what extent is BPM positioned to expand into Southeast Asia in a way that can protect the company's intellectual property?

1. What assumptions must persist to maintain the validity of the most likely outcome?	2. How strongly does the data support the inference's estimated probability? (1–10)	3. What is the level of confidence in the data? (1–10)	4. Would this assumption's failure cause any others to fail? (1–10)	5. What is the impact on the inference's estimated probability if the assumption doesn't hold?
1. Potential partner's reputation for honesty and performance check out	6	6	7	9
2. Local labor force can be vetted	7	8	7	7
3. Courts enforce intellectual property violations	8	8	8	9

4. There is a growing market for our product line	8	8	6	7
5. Intellectual property laws sufficiently protect proprietary processes	8	8	8	8
6. Our computer security systems are sufficient to thwart insider threats	6	8	10	10
One too many				

Figure 19. The Task Force's completed KAC awaits analysis.

Task Force Next Looks for Patterns in the Data and Identifies Linchpins

The stakes for the company are high. The length and depth of the discussions were sobering and often difficult, as members sorted through each Key Assumption's potential impact on the inference's estimated probability and selection of the linchpins. The Task Force understood that the story was in the numbers, but they needed to draw it out. To help start the process, the Task Force facilitator assigned the members to collectively answer the following three questions based on their KAC ratings and to report back to the group.

The Task Force was instructed to answer the questions in full sentences using the data. Their responses will be shown in Chapter 10. How they answer them will determine how they refine their lead inference.

- Where is the Task Force's lead inference most vulnerable? Identify the linchpins. Explain using the data.
- What are other important vulnerabilities the Task Force now needs to consider? Explain using the data.

- Where does the Task Force think its assessment is on comparatively secure footing? Explain using the data.

EXERCISE: For Your Product Complete the KAC Framework

Instructions:

Turn to the Workbook Chapter 9.

Try to work with at least one colleague to discuss your ratings decisions, which is a good opportunity to collaborate. Recall that column 5 is not an average of columns 2–4.

Insert the Key Assumptions selected for your product listed in Chapter 8 in no particular order.

To complete the exercise use the framework in the Workbook—recall it is a Word document designed to be downloaded so you can work with it as a separate document to make reviewing and editing easier. Fill in the template with ratings. This part can be done independently but the power of the KAC rests in the discussions about the ratings. We suggest listing them randomly vs. any sort of rank order to avoid biasing your ratings. Along the way ask yourself how a KAC exercise might also help you manage your collaboration challenge.

Then stop. We will pick up the story in Chapter 10, where the KAC ratings are processed.

CHAPTER TEN

Select Linchpin Assumptions, Estimate Most Likely Outcome and Implications, Mitigate Risk, Manage Dissent

GOAL: Based on examples from the BPM Task Force's exercises, apply the results of your KAC exercise in Chapter 9 to develop the last four elements of your B.L.U.F. that shift the *Intelligent Analysis* process from What's Known to What's Next.

Note: This is a long chapter with multiple exercises that include the last four B.L.U.F. elements. It begins with how the Task Force selected their Linchpin Assumptions, estimated the Most Likely Outcome, determined the implications, and proposed ways to mitigate risks. It closes with a section on the challenges of managing differences in a collaborative exercise like the Task Force's.

The exercises are enumerated step by step (1-7) in the text and then in the Workbook, but once you have read through each step, all the work should be done in the Workbook, referring back to the text for models. Step 7 completes the component parts of your B.L.U.F. At that point we will ask you to revise the draft B.L.U.F. framework started in Chapter 6.

Key Learning Objectives

At the end of this chapter, analysts will be better able to:

- Apply the results of your KAC exercise in Chapter 9 to complete the steps necessary to finalize your B.L.U.F.
- Manage integrating dissenting views into analytic products.

In this chapter we pick up the Task Force's next steps as they shape their assessment of the risks to BPM's G-codes if a plant is built in Southeast Asia. At this point, they have completed their KAC and begun the process of looking for patterns that emerge from the ratings. The Task Force's review of their KAC ratings will determine how they answer the facilitator's three questions that will be the basis for how they complete last the four B.L.U.F. elements. The Task Force's answers are in the data and their expertise.

A reminder: the purpose of the last four elements is to assess the accuracy of the Board's optimistic (highly likely) estimated probability of success that answers the senior managers' KIQ.

The last four B.L.U.F. elements include:

- **The most likely outcome.** How close the Linchpin Assumptions are to a fact are the most important drivers that will explain to the consumer the likelihood that their desired state or an event or development will occur, in addition to the range of other possible outcomes.
- **Implications for the consumer (the so what of the so what).** How the most likely outcome impacts the consumer's path to the desired outcome.
- **Mitigation strategies.** Steps that can be taken to address the most important vulnerabilities to improve the estimated probability that the desired outcome or an event or development will occur.
- **Indicators to gauge the strategies' effectiveness.**

(Drawn from: *Tradecraft Primer*, 2009; Davis 1997; Heuer 1999)

To help you track your progress we have numbered each of the steps. They are cited in both the book and the Workbook.

1. Assess patterns in the data to answer the facilitator's three questions.
2. Determine the Linchpin Assumptions.
3. Explain the Most Likely Outcome.
4. Gauge the LOC in the Most Likely Outcome.
5. Explain the implications of the Most Likely Outcome.
6. Develop mitigation strategies to address vulnerabilities.
7. Develop indicators to gauge their effectiveness.

EXAMPLE: The Task Force Completes Their KAC

The Task Force's approved KIQ: To what extent is BPM positioned to expand into Southeast Asia in a way that can protect the company's intellectual property?

The draft response: Reliable reporting which documents inconsistent legal protections for intellectual property, and a high-risk cyber threat environment in Southeast Asia, indicate that, although BPM can open a plant there, our software is *highly* vulnerable to insider threats, and the Task Force recommends assessing potential mitigation strategies before deciding to move forward.

For clarity, Figure 20 below repeats the Task Force's completed KAC from Chapter 9.

1. What assumptions must persist to maintain the validity of the most likely outcome?	2. How strongly does the data support the inference's estimated probability? (1–10)	3. What is the level of confidence in the data? (1–10)	4. Would this assumption's failure cause any others to fail? (1–10)	5. What is the impact on the inference's estimated probability if the assumption doesn't hold?
1. Potential partner's reputation for honesty and performance check out	6	6	7	9
2. Local labor force can be vetted	7	8	7	7
3. Courts enforce intellectual property violations	8	8	8	9
4. There is a growing market for our product line	8	8	6	7
5. Intellectual property laws sufficiently protect proprietary processes	8	8	8	8
6. Our computer security systems are sufficient to thwart insider threats	6	8	10	10
One too many				

Figure 20. KAC results provide critical insights into BPM's probability of success.

Step 1: BPM Assesses Patterns in the Data to Answer Facilitator's Three Questions

The completed KAC is rich in insights. The facilitator guided the Task Force through a series of structured data-driven discussions focused on answering the three questions posed at the end of Chapter 9, drawing on expertise from across the company. You will see how, in completing the last four B.L.U.F. elements, the Task Force will depend heavily on the level of detail in their responses. In the example, the Task Force members first explain their reasoning then express the answers in the form of an inference.

Here are the Task Force's responses:

1) Where is the Board of Directors' Task Force's lead inference most vulnerable?

Identify the Linchpin Assumptions. Explain using the data, then express the response as an inference.

Explanations:

- The Task Force finally agreed that assumptions 3 (courts enforce intellectual property violations) and 6 (our computer security systems are sufficient to thwart insider threats) were the two Linchpin Assumptions. The decision was not surprising; BPM had spent years and millions of dollars developing and refining both the machinery and the codes that drove them. Losing control of their intellectual property in an environment with an uneven record of enforcing intellectual property rights would threaten BPM's long-term viability, if not bring about its collapse. They knew of multiple examples where companies that expanded into Southeast Asia found some of their most important trade secrets showing up in other firm's products with only limited legal recourse.

Responses expressed as inferences:

- *Assumption 3:* A review of publicly available court decisions and direct trial transcripts reveals that the court ruled against the US company in over 60 percent of the cases, which indicates that we would be *unlikely* to prevail in efforts to prosecute violators or seek any remedy for intellectual property theft.

- *Assumption 6:* Drawing on a range of data on cyber risks in Southeast Asia and assessing BPM's current cyber security program are *highly likely* to show that BPM's codes are vulnerable to insider and external threats and that BPM will be unable to defend its systems over the longer term.

2) What other important vulnerabilities does the Board of Directors need to consider?

Explain using the data and then express the response as an inference.

The Task Force decided that Assumption 1 (potential partner's reputation for honesty and performance check out) and Assumption 5 (national intellectual property laws sufficiently protect proprietary processes) also pose risks.

Explanations:

- *Assumption 1:* The impact on the initiative of a poor choice of partner is significant, but in selecting a local partner there are multiple sources, including media and other clients' experiences, to draw on. Moreover, there is a considerable number of local US-based companies that can assist in finding a suitable partner or firm to assist in the process.

- *Assumption 5:* The body of intellectual-property-related law is extensive and provides important protections for a range of intellectual property with a court system devoted to enforcing the laws. In practice, however, the legislators have often been criticized in the press and among local US-based businesses for changing the rules to discriminate against foreign companies. Moreover, the changes have created loopholes and exceptions and give judges wide latitude in enforcing them.

Responses expressed as inferences:

- *Assumption 1:* A review of potential partners drawn from experiences of other US-based companies and local resources indicates that BPM is likely to find a partner that will help the company navigate local laws and maintain awareness of developments that could impact the company.

- *Assumption 5:* A review of intellectual-property-related court decisions and discussions with US-based law firms operating in Southeast Asia indicates that in over 60 percent of cases, appeals courts reversed rulings favorable to US companies, indicating that BPM will be unlikely to find legal redress in any regional court.

3) Where does the Task Force think its assessment is on comparatively secure footing?

Explain using the data then express the response as an inference.

Explanation: The Task Force agreed that Assumptions 2 (local labor force can be vetted) and 4 (there is an expandable market for our product line) were on comparatively secure footing.

Responses expressed as inferences:

- *Assumption 2:* The region has multiple recruiting companies that can draw on a deep pool of skilled workers with track records at other companies. Those recruiting firms would also be likely to help with the vetting.

- *Assumption 4:* The extensive Southeast Asia market together with BPM's already established network of customers indicates that BPM is highly likely to continue expanding its regional sales.

EXERCISE: Assess Patterns in the Data to Answer the Facilitator's Three Questions

Instructions:

Turn to the Workbook Chapter 10, Step 1.

Use the Task Force's responses as a model and answer the same three questions which the facilitator posed to them for your product.

Step 2: BPM Task Force Determines Their Linchpin Assumptions

As indicated in the Task Force's response to question 1, Key Assumptions 3 (courts enforce intellectual property violations) and 6 (our computer security systems are sufficient to thwart insider threats) were the two Linchpin Assumptions. The Task Force also decided that Key Assumption 1 (potential partner's reputation for honesty and performance check out) and Key Assumption 5 (intellectual property laws sufficiently protect proprietary processes) also pose risks.

EXERCISE: Determine the Linchpin Assumptions

Instructions:

Turn to the Workbook Chapter 10, Step 2.

Use the Task Force's reasoning for their Linchpin selections as a model and choose your Linchpin Assumptions.

Step 3: BPM Task Force Develops the Most Likely Outcome

For the BPM Task Force the "so what"—the most likely outcome—is starting to take shape. Note how the analysis is data-driven and firmly anchored in BPM's KAC ratings, as well as in the Task Force members' own expertise and experience. They used the same construct (A + B → C) to express their revised outlook as an inference. Most important, they made sure the caveat used was consistent with the data. The assessment meets the three important standards: it is transparent, defensible, and traceable.

EXERCISE: Develop the Most Likely Outcome

Instructions:

Turn to the Workbook Chapter 10, Step 3.

Using the Task Force's example as a model, revise your lead inference.

Step 4: BPM Task Force Gauges the Level of Confidence (LOC) in the Most Likely Outcome

BPM used the guides and Source Assessment Framework to develop their LOC that follows the lead inference: We have only moderate confidence in our assessment because the data on the challenges and opportunities that come with deciding to move forward varies widely, but, overall, well-documented loopholes in the legal framework, and a mixed record of court decisions raise concerns about transparency and BPM's ability to protect its interests.

EXERCISE: Gauge the Level of Confidence in the Most Likely Outcome

Instructions:

Turn to the Workbook Chapter 10, Step 4.

Using the Task Force's example as a model, draft your LOC statement as the second sentence of your revised lead inference.

Step 5: BPM Task Force Explains Implications of the Most Likely Outcome

The "so what of the so what" explains how the most likely outcome potentially impacts whether your consumer will reach their desired state or whether the event or development will occur.

Among Task Force members, discussion over the implications for the senior managers and the Board of Directors was intense, ranging from qualified support for the Southeast Asia plant to outright opposition. Indeed, while the majority of the Task Force saw at least a potential way forward, two members did not see a safe path ahead under any circumstances and wanted to find alternatives that would avoid opening a plant in Southeast Asia and still allow BPM to expand its market. They asked for the opportunity to have their views clarified and presented to the senior managers. More on that later.

Some ground rules for developing the implications of your most likely outcome:

- The implications need to be rooted in the data. And it is here, and later in developing mitigation strategies, where expertise and collaboration are critical.
- Implications can be developed drawing from the deep expertise of the Task Force, but other useful insights may well come from the experiences of other companies that have successfully—or not—started similar companies in the region. For example, other US-based companies in Southeast Asia or the local American Chamber of Commerce would be especially helpful.

To illustrate how the implications flow from the most likely outcome, we repeat below the Task Force's look ahead followed by their agreed-upon implications:

- Reliable data documents inconsistent legal protections for intellectual property, and a high-risk cyber threat environment in Southeast Asia indicates that, although BPM can open a plant there, our software is highly vulnerable to insider threats, and the Task Force recommends assessing potential mitigation strategies before deciding to move forward. We have only moderate confidence in our assessment because the data on the challenges and opportunities that come with deciding to move forward varies widely, but, overall, well-documented loopholes in the legal framework and a mixed record of court decisions raise concerns about transparency and BPM's ability to protect their interests.

The implications:

- Strategic decisions will require deeper regional expertise in cyber security and local copyright enforcement and stronger relationships with local US-based businesses and law firms.
- To ensure that BPM meets its overall goal of expanding its market share in Southeast Asia and protecting our intellectual property, begin to explore alternatives to locating our new plant there.
- BPM must vet and contract with a local partner to assess the operating environment and facilitate permitting and other bureaucratic requirements.

EXERCISE: Explain the Implications of the Most Likely Outcome

Instructions:

Turn to the Workbook Chapter 10, Step 5.

Using the Task Force's example as a model, list at least three implications of your recast assessment of the most likely outcome.

Step 6: BPM Task Force Develops Mitigation Strategies to Address Vulnerabilities

> **Note**: Mitigation strategies and indicators are described separately as Steps 6 and 7, but because they are so closely related we created a combined SAT—Mitigation and Indicator Framework—which is used below.

Intelligent Analysis is about identifying and managing risk and navigating uncertainty, not avoiding it. Only the consumers—in this case the senior managers and the Board of Directors—can determine their organization's risk tolerance. The senior managers, in fact, agreed with the results of the KAC exercise and reported the Task Force's findings to the Board of Directors. They explained the process and made clear that, except for two dissenters, the Task Force assessed that a safe plant was still possible.

The Board of Directors agreed with the assessment and decided to slow down. But at the same time, with an already existing customer base and other ready advantages, they still insisted that expanding into Southeast Asia remained a priority for long-term growth. Stepping away was not an option. With that, the Board of Directors asked the senior managers to turn the Task Force to creating a path that mitigated the risk from the two most critical vulnerabilities: the legal system and insider threats to their software. The Board, especially BPM's founding members, also wanted to make sure they recognized the dissenting views by hearing the outliers' perspectives.

To meet the board's requirement for a path forward the Task Force decided to complete Steps 6 and 7 in tandem and display them in a table that clearly linked the strategies to the indicators. While discussed separately, mitigation strategies and indicators are so closely related that, in addition to discussing them as a single step, we created an SAT that combines both steps, the Mitigation and Indicator Framework, shown below and in the Workbook. Together this SAT helps analysts be more deliberate and thorough in thinking about risk.

Mitigating Most Critical Risks First

The facilitator was still helping the Task Force and focused them first on the two Linchpin Assumptions. The facilitator also reminded them to avoid falling back on using a conditional vocabulary to caveat their suggestions. The words *could, might, may,* and *should* add no value without the required follow-on "because…" that would explain with data.

Again, while expertise within the Task Force was important, the Task Force also drew on multiple other sources that had experience in the region. To start, the Task Force developed another KIQ to guide their Southeast Asia strategy:

- To what extent are the experiences of other similar companies applicable to managing the initiative's key vulnerabilities and meeting BPM's requirements?

With their new KIQ they homed in on US Government data, the American Chambers of Commerce in the region, and multiple experts in the US and Southeast Asia on how other companies prepared themselves to deal with cyber security, intellectual property protections, and the legal system. The results of the Task Force's deliberations are in Figure 21 in the next section.

EXERCISE: Develop Mitigation Strategies to Address Vulnerabilities

Instructions:

Turn to the Workbook Chapter 10, Step 6.

Using the Task Force's example as a model, develop mitigation strategies for each assumption included in your responses to the facilitator's first two questions and insert them in columns 1 and 2 of the Mitigation and Indicator Framework.

Step 7: Develop Indicators of the Strategies' Effectiveness

Indicators guard against surprises but are often overlooked or done poorly. We want to dive more deeply into the use of indicators because, while primarily working in tandem with mitigation strategies, they are also important in their own right. Indeed, developing indicators is a widely respected sub-specialty among the US intelligence services. And we will see from the Task Force's example below that they can play the same role in the private sector. Specifically, indicators can do the following:

- **Track the "health" of the other assumptions**. Beyond monitoring the Linchpin Assumptions, indicators can be a check on complacency. Assumptions that look like a safe bet now can change quickly or more slowly over the longer term.

- **Help analysts manage differences.** Rather than remain at loggerheads, teams can develop indicators that monitor shifting trend lines. Equally important, clearly written indicators can explain the potential for a wider range of possible outcomes. Because of the fault lines among and between the Board and senior managers, for example, the Task Force decided to develop indicators as one way to keep the senior managers and the Board informed of any changes in intellectual property protection, the legal system, or the status of other US companies in Southeast Asia.

Over the longer term a set of indicators can do the following:

- **Point out changes in the operating environment.** These shifts can include, for example, business and competitive intelligence, new product announcements, insider threats, mergers and acquisitions, and cyberattacks. For organizations with overseas interests, warnings can include labor and political unrest and multiple legal issues.

- **Assess longer-term trends.** These can include developments that would impact BPM's potential operating environment, such as new competitors entering the market, developments in labor markets, demographic shifts, and legislation and compliance issues.
- **Help update assessments.** Indicators' role will be especially important as technical and informant data add more data points to a very early assessment. For example, as possible outcomes surface, indicators can help track shifting trends.

The facilitator asks that the Task Force use the Mitigation and Indicator Framework, shown in the table below, to do their work, combining Steps 6 and 7 to underscore their importance in managing risks (Ramsey 1995).

EXAMPLE: Task Force Uses Mitigation and Indicator Framework to Plan and Measure Mitigation Strategies' Effectiveness

Below in Figure 21 is the result of their work based on their selected Key Assumptions. Note the indicators' specific actions and the clarity of the strategies and metrics that gauge what works and what does not.

For example:

- Not helpful: Hire locally to staff the plant / BPM fails to hire local employees.

Instead:

- Metric-driven: Hire eight vetted local managers within 90 days.

1) Linchpin Assumption	2) Possible Mitigation Strategies	3) Indicators that Steps are Working	4) Indicators that Steps are Not Working	5) Comments
3. Courts enforce intellectual property violations.	▪ Explore alternative sites/solutions that meet Board goals and also protect G-Codes. ▪ Hire a local law firm known for protecting intellectual property in courts, as well as compliance with patent and trademark laws.	At least one year before final approval: ▪ Alternative sites/solutions that meet goals developed and reviewed. ▪ A local legal firm contracted to identify local partner and BPM's patents and copyrights legally registered.	▪ Locally hired legal firm reportedly colluding with rival companies and courts. ▪ Critical documents not yet registered.	▪ Even if local intellectual property protections are well validated, navigating the system is a challenge beyond what a local business partner can provide.
6. Our computer security systems are sufficient to thwart insider threats.	At least one year before final approval: ▪ Contract a US cyber security firm to assess BPM's systems and develop a mitigation strategy.	At least one year before construction begins: ▪ Upgraded BPM cyber security system meets requirements to protect the G-Codes. ▪ Qualified technical personnel and support staff identified and vetted.	▪ More than ten violations of cyber security protocols in thirty-day period. ▪ More than two local employees terminated for attempting to steal codes.	▪ Outside experts can assess the magnitude of the risks and possible solutions (if any) that can facilitate a safe move abroad.

Figure 21. Task Force pairing of mitigation strategies and indicators.

What the columns mean:

Column 1: **The vulnerability.** What makes this a Linchpin Assumption? Reading across the row in the KAC, write out one or two sentences that describe why it is especially vulnerable.

Column 2: **The mitigation strategy.** Describe specifically what action will be taken.

Column 3: **Indicators that the strategy is working.** Think of it this way: What would we expect to see if the strategy results in a positive change in the Linchpin Assumption? The indicators are expressed as metrics based on observable data.

Column 4: **Indicators that the strategy is not working.** Again, expressed in metrics. The actual metrics and observations matter because they help avoid just expressing them as opposites. Above are examples for correctly completing columns 3 and 4.

Column 5: **Comments.** Included here are observations about the strategy or the metrics.

EXERCISE: Add Indicators to Gauge the Strategies' Effectiveness from Step 6

Instructions:

Turn to the Workbook Chapter 10, Step 7.

Using the Task Force's example as a model, insert indicators and comments for the mitigation strategies which you identified in Step 6 in columns 3, 4 and 5 of the Mitigation and Indicator Framework.

Dissents Open New Perspectives, Strengthen Assessments

In the BPM example it is not surprising that, given the significant risks to the company, there would be Task Force members who simply opposed the initiative. The dissenters agreed that the plant could be built, but this is a high-stakes decision, and the plant is only part of the equation. The risk to the computer systems and inconsistent legal systems posed an unacceptable threat to BPM. For this reason, they saw the mitigation strategies as insufficient and wanted the managers to recommend an alternative approach to expanding BPM's market expansion into Southeast Asia.

- As one alternative they suggested moving closer to the region, perhaps the West Coast, Hawaii, or even Japan, or building secure warehouse facilities to support larger inventories in Southeast Asia. Their point was that, given the lack of transparency in the legal system and the ongoing risk of insider threats, there was no safe path.

- The dissenters wanted the Task Force's assessment to recognize that the company over the long term could not defend its intellectual property in Southeast Asia. It recommended that the Task Force develop an expansion plan that achieved both goals: an expanding market and protecting the very heart of the company's success.

Note that, although they were disagreeing with the Task Force's assessment, they were still respecting the process. These were dissenters, not process wreckers. They disagreed that the data are sufficient to support the assessment at the expressed level of certainty. They made other suggestions as well (see below).

In *Intelligent Analysis*, dissents need to be as carefully managed as any other phase of the analytic process.

- Disagreements over assessments are frequent and expected among intelligence analysts and their organizations more broadly (Heuer 2009).

- As explained earlier, at their roots are differences over the validity of the underlying assumptions that support the inference: what caveat (*likely/unlikely, highly likely/unlikely,....*), best characterizes the relationship between the facts and what can be inferred from the facts.

- Sometimes the disagreements are so deep that they need to be expressed in the form of formal written dissents. But their comments must be data-driven and clearly written; simply disagreeing doesn't count. A clear delineation of differences is important information for consumers, and dissents must follow the same rules.

- Dissents vary in length but are more typically expressed in relatively short paragraphs, something like:

  - The Task Force's senior cyber security and outside legal experts with long experience in Southeast Asia agree that the Task Force's assessment should more definitively state that from their perspective there is no safe path that meets their long-term goals and that other approaches should be explored.

- Weaknesses in the legal system will limit BPM's ability to protect its codes and processes.
- The cyber expert added that no cyber security plan is a match for a hacker's technical prowess, and the ever-evolving tools available to hackers will quickly outstrip BPM's protection capabilities.
- Task Force members focusing on hiring added that, while the hiring pool is large, finding qualified staff that meet vetting requirements would also be a challenge. Transferring US-based managers to oversee the startup and hiring would be two steps to take to mitigate staffing and management concerns.

Dissents Need to be Encouraged

Intelligent Analysis recognizes that such data-driven dissents are one of our process's most important strengths. Encouraging differences and recording them as dissents, and giving the rationale behind them, are essential to the transparency that bolsters the credibility of the Task Force's assessment when it is presented to consumers. In fact, SAT's collaborative environment encourages disagreements that can be expressed as dissents. In the case of BPM, the range of risks involved merited deeper discussion about whether a potential path would be possible. After reviewing the dissent, the senior managers decided to integrate their views into the lead inference. It now reads:

> While BPM will be able to open a plant in Southeast Asia, multiple sources indicate the company is unlikely to be able to protect its intellectual property against insider threats, and the Task Force recommends the Board of Directors step back from the initiative while managers investigate whether there is an alternate approach that would facilitate BPM's market expansion in the region; two *Task Force members, however, assess that no such path exists and suggest other approaches to meeting the Board of Directors' desired outcome.*

This paragraph would replace the lead inference in the B.L.U.F. Make sure to recast the entire paragraph to align with the updated assessment.

Dissents Need to be Managed: Scenario Downplayed Real World Tensions

Our BPM scenario played out smoothly—too smoothly in fact to mirror what generally happens in diverse groups trying to solve tough problems, whether under pressure or not. Our story was set up to illustrate how the process should unfold, albeit in an ideal environment. For example:

- The Board of Directors was serious about the review, which reflects a not-so- common corporate culture.
- Task Force members supported the approach and accepted the ground rules.
- The Task Force facilitator was trained, understood the process, and kept the Task Force focused. The leader managed dissent and avoided organizational silence. Everyone's voice was heard.

In reality, however, all three conditions are rarely evident. Unlike BPM's senior managers and Board members, decision makers are often reluctant to cede authority or are just looking for support for their own positions. The challenge here may well be operating in a culture where analysts are poorly understood and where they may well simply regard such exercises as merely exercises. Even when analysts provide well-documented assessments, this does little to ensure they will be welcomed or followed, which ultimately is their customer's own decision.

Guard the Process

As for the Task Force members, more often than not there is at least one participant with critical expertise who does not believe in SATs, likes the old ways of decision analysis, and sits back with arms folded. Others may be more vocal, touting their seniority and experience and just as often clinging to their assumptions regardless of the data.

To be clear, disruptors are not dissenters, but rather in fact pose more substantive, and serious, risks to the *Intelligent Analysis* process. These rifts frequently surface within colllaborative analytic initiatives and, if not understood as disruptions versus dissent and managed as such, will undermine a balanced assessment. Task Force facilitators can help in this regard, but it is also analysts' responsibility to keep the discussions focused on the data and enforce the process.

The risks are too great for the consumer to skip or not follow the steps. The most common disruptions include the following:

- **Pressure to go beyond the data.** Inferences drawn from inferences are endemic, especially when the information base is thin. It can come from anyone in the group, but again most often the culprits are senior analysts who tout expertise and long experience and are convinced of their brilliance. SATs are meant to structure discussions and shift them away from personalities to the data. Push back.

- **Misuse of conditional caveats.** Recall that "because" must follow conditional caveats such as might, could, may, should, and maybe to transform speculation into an informed explanation of other possible outcomes. Force the issue with Task Force members who want to do otherwise.

- **Probability drift.** Endless arguments and fatigue breed compromise. The back-and-forth can lead to changes in the estimated probability at different points in the text, which is why the Task Force needs to revisit the entire text to ensure that decision-makers see a consistent message.

- **Judgment creep.** Similarly, analysts need to pay attention to what one CIA officer calls "judgment creep," when a past carefully caveated judgment unconsciously becomes a firmer judgment over time.

Intelligent Analysis can also help analysts avoid two other serious risks to the process: overconfidence and unwarranted caution.

- **Overconfidence** most often shows up as just plain arrogance. Someone in the room pushes for an unwarranted and unsupportable probability estimate, often with a raised voice, claims of deep experience, "just a gut instinct," or all of the above. If analysts opt to fold, be forewarned. Analysts are trading the safe harbor of *Intelligent Analysis* for a minefield where analysis becomes prediction and creates a ready path over the next cliff.

- **Unwarranted caution** is at the other end of the analytic spectrum and is just as potentially dangerous. In these cases, analysts pull punches to avoid being wrong. "Probably" is the most overused word in *Intelligent Analysis*. It is supposed to be used only to signal that there are other possible outcomes, which is part of the process, but it is too often used as a hedge. Trouble arises when the estimated probability is lowered despite a strong evidentiary base built on high-quality data. This behavior can leave decision makers wondering what they are missing. If there are alternative outcomes, explain them.

The big takeaway from this very long chapter

Intelligent Analysis is not a silver bullet, and all analysts fall short at some time in their careers. But being wrong despite careful attention to the process—for what we call the right reasons—is OK. By this we mean it is sufficient if the analysis, to repeat once again, is transparent, defensible, and repeatable and if analysts are able to walk consumers through their reasoning. These challenges are what make *Intelligent Analysis* so important. It is the hard work of being an analyst. The tradecraft is a shield, not from being wrong but from wrong thinking and from skipping or skimming some steps. So stick to the script. Be methodical at every step; Resist "making a call" that goes beyond the reporting. It feels great until the phone rings. And it will.

Finalize Your B.L.U.F. Framework

You have now developed all the elements of the B.L.U.F. including a revised title and lead inference. In this exercise we complete the draft B.L.U.F. framework from Chapter 6. Below in Figure 22 is the Task Force's finalized B.L.U.F. framework including the title and revised lead inference.

EXAMPLE: Task Force's Finalized B.L.U.F. Framework

Title	Board's Southeast Asia Initiative: Plant Looks Good, Intellectual Property at Risk
Inference that Captures the B.L.U.F.	Reliable data document inconsistent legal protections for intellectual property, and a high-risk cyber threat environment in Southeast Asia indicates that, although BPM can open a plant there, our software is highly vulnerable to insider threats. We have moderate confidence in our assessment, because the data on the challenges and opportunities that come with deciding to move forward varies widely but, overall, well-documented loopholes in the legal framework and a mixed record of court decisions raise concerns about transparency and BPM's ability to protect our interests, so we recommend further analysis of the risks and potential mitigation strategies.
New Development ("what")	The Board of Directors wants to open a manufacturing facility in Southeast Asia and estimates the initiative is *highly likely* to succeed; the senior managers disagree.
Why Now?	The Board sees a growing market and their own analysis of Southeast Asia shows the company's proprietary software can be protected against insider threats.
How Does It Work?	The Board of Directors wants to use a local partner to help BPM navigate the bureaucracy and related challenges to opening the plant.
What is the Impact So Far?	No decision has been made, and the Board agreed with the senior managers to establish a Task Force to assess potential vulnerabilities.
What's Next? ("so what")	The Task Force reported to the senior managers that, while the plant can certainly be built, the company's software would be *highly* vulnerable to insider threats.
What are the Implications for the Consumer ("so what of the so what")?	A final decision will require deeper regional expertise in cyber security and local patents and copyright enforcement, stronger relationships with local firms and a comprehensive assessment of BPM's cyber security programs.
Potential Mitigation Steps and Indicators of Strategies' Effectiveness	To manage the risks, at least one year ahead of final approval a local law firm should be hired, partner(s) selected, copyrights registered, alternative sites evaluated, a validated cyber security plan in place and vetted technical personnel in place.

Figure 22. The Task Force's finalized B.L.U.F. framework

EXERCISE: Finalize Your B.L.U.F. Framework

Instructions:

Turn to Chapter 10 in the Workbook to the blank B.L.U.F. Framework.

- Copy the entries from your draft B.L.U.F. framework in Chapter 6, then revise the last four elements with the results of your work in Chapters 7-9 and the exercises which you completed in Steps 1-7.
- Revise the lead inference and title.
- Use BPM's example as a model.

CHAPTER ELEVEN

Refine, Expand Your B.L.U.F. Sweep Text for Errors

"The main thing I try to do is write as clearly as I can. I rewrite a good deal to make it clear."

—E.B. White, *Elements of Style*

"Good writing should be transparent, like a windowpane."

—George Orwell, *Why I Write*

GOAL: To understand that a carefully crafted B.L.U.F. can provide the framework for longer analytic products, what to include in a three-point summary, and the importance of careful proofreading to bolster the product's credibility.

Key Learning Objectives

At the end of this chapter analysts will be better able to:

- Convert the B.L.U.F framework into a standalone paragraph that delivers a complete answer to the consumer's Key Intelligence Question.
- Expand the B.L.U.F. into an internally consistent product of any length.
- Draft a three-point summary of longer assessments that answer the KIQ.
- Apply the Four Sweeps technique to review drafts and two other techniques for self-reviewing assessments. (This chapter is drawn from Cariens 2012 and James 2009.)

Complete the Deliverable

With the framework completed, in this exercise the finalized B.L.U.F. elements become complete sentences in the standalone paragraph, like they did for the draft B.L.U.F. at the end of Chapter 6.

Below is the BPM Task Force's assessment delivered to their senior managers that can serve as a model. Note how it essentially duplicates the Task Force's finalized B.L.U.F. framework example in Chapter 10.

EXAMPLE: The Task Force Deliverable to the Senior Managers

Board's Southeast Asia Initiative: Plant Looks Good, Intellectual Property at Risk

The Board of Directors wants to open a manufacturing facility in Southeast Asia and estimates the initiative is highly likely to succeed; the senior managers disagree. The Board sees a growing market and their own analysis of Southeast Asia shows the company's proprietary software can be protected against insider threats. The Board of Directors wants to use a local partner to help BPM navigate the bureaucracy and related challenges to opening the plant. No decision has been made, and the Board agreed with the senior managers to establish a Task Force to assess potential vulnerabilities. The Task Force reported to the senior managers that, while the plant can certainly be built, the company's software would be highly vulnerable to insider threats. A final decision will require deeper regional expertise in cyber security and local patent and copyright enforcement, stronger relationships with local firms and a comprehensive assessment of BPM's cyber security programs. To manage these risks, at least one year ahead of final approval a local law firm should be hired, partner(s) selected, patents and copyrights registered, alternative sites evaluated, a validated cyber security plan in place and vetted technical personnel hired. Two analysts dissented from the assessment, stating that there is no safe path and that they want the Task Force to look for alternative approaches.

EXERCISE: Complete the Deliverable

Instructions:

Turn to Chapter 11 in the Workbook. Using the BPM example as a model, copy the entries from your B.L.U.F. framework into a standalone paragraph. And stop. You will have opportunities to review and revise the text in the following exercises before delivering it to your consumer.

B.L.U.F. Shapes Longer Analytic Products

A strong title and well-crafted B.L.U.F alone are good for a quick summary for busy readers. But for those readers needing more depth and detail, the B.L.U.F. structure gives analysts a framework for building a multi-paragraph story. Specifically, each sentence in the B.L.U.F. can be easily expanded into a paragraph. To make this format work, each sentence can be reformulated as a Sub-question that answers the KIQ. The standard in *Intelligent Analysis* is answering the Sub-question with no more than three data points. For example:

- What is the new development/trend/insight?
- Why now? What is driving the development or issue?
- How does it work (the mechanics)?
- What is the impact so far?
- What is next?

- What are the implications of the outcome: the "so what of the so what"?
- What mitigation strategies can sustain/change outlook?
- What are some indicators that a mitigation strategy is working?

EXAMPLE: BPM Task Force Expands Their B.L.U.F.

Note the structure used below.

Title: Proposed Southeast Asia Expansion: Insider Threats Pose High Risk to BPM's Intellectual Property

What is the new development driving the requirement?

The BPM Board of Directors wants to open a manufacturing facility in Southeast Asia.

You need just three data points from the data for each paragraph. The US intelligence services reason that analysts will often use multiple sources to support their lead. Such data dumps might make you feel like you are being helpful and cautious in setting out your argument, but consumers can get bogged down in denser detail, and the changing paragraph length makes it hard for consumers to navigate—deliver it the same way every time. Three is enough. If needed, use tables, charts, or textboxes to cover any other important points.

- Data
- Data
- Data

Why is this development or event occurring now?

The Board of Directors sees this as an important opportunity to expand into a lucrative market and is confident that the company's intellectual property will be protected against insider threats.

- Data
- Data
- Data

And so on . . . .

This approach to leveraging your B.L.U.F. has important advantages. Most important, it gives analysts a skeleton outline and standardized format and structure, which makes expanding the B.L.U.F. faster and easier. It also separates thinking from drafting, avoids excessive citations, and under time pressure allows farming out specific sections to relevant experts. Moreover, reviewing just the lead inferences tests coherence and clarity of message and allows reviewers to quickly review the structure and recommend changes before drafting begins. If the assessment has section headings or subtitles, they also need to be analytic and align with the B.L.U.F. They should capture the main point of the section in three to five words. This internal alignment will help busy readers follow the story just by reading the assessment at any level, including just the title, the B.L.U.F. subheads, or topic sentences.

For example, the subsection on why the Board of Directors Now Sees New Opportunities in Asia Southeast Asia.

EXERCISE: B.L.U.F. Shapes Longer Analytic Products

Instructions:

Turn to Chapter 11 in the Workbook.

- Use the outline provided to show how you would expand your lead paragraph into a five- or six-paragraph product.
- When completed make sure to review for flow and consistency with the lead inference and paragraph—note the connective tissue.

A Summary Can Determine Impact

Rule of thumb: Any assessment over two pages requires a summary because it may well be the only part read after the title. Summaries convey the B.L.U.F.'s key message in three ticks (or bullets) of no more than 8–10 words per tick. Using this format makes the summary easier to read and understand more quickly than a standard prose paragraph. It can be drawn from language from your inference or the B.L.U.F.; repetition is acceptable.

EXAMPLE: A Summary of BPM's Task Force Report

- Although BPM can open a plant in Southeast Asia the Task Force assesses that our software is highly vulnerable to insider threats.

- The Task Force has already started developing potential mitigation strategies to address the most important vulnerabilities and will report soon.
- We have only moderate confidence in our assessment because data on the challenges and opportunities that come with deciding to move forward varies widely, so we have also stepped-up collection in the region to fill important gaps.

EXERCISE: Develop a Summary for Your Longer Product

Rule of thumb: Any assessment over two pages requires a summary. Summaries convey the same message as the title and B.L.U.F. key message in three ticks (or bullets) of no more than 8–10 words per tick.

Instructions:

Turn to Chapter 11 in the Workbook.

Think about what the consumer needs to take away from your product. Looking at your title, inference, and B.L.U.F., develop a summary of the key points in three ticks; repetition from the text is acceptable.

Here is the format:

- Bullet one:
- Bullet two:
- Bullet three:

The Four Sweeps Process Facilitates Self-Reviewing Process

Nothing should leave your desk until it is truly done. If you feel relieved to be done, you are putting your work and hard thinking and reputation at risk. Time pressure can be a constraint but leave time to review the text or ask a colleague to help. Skipping this step and sending a poorly proofed text is worse than being ten minutes late, which will not be remembered at all. One manager told Jay when the phone calls started coming about the deadline that "20 minutes won't kill them." Consumers may see inconsistencies and errors in grammar and spelling as indicators that other elements of the assessment are also likely to be flawed, and they will hunt for them.

The Four Sweeps review approach breaks down into four parts the process of reviewing your work. This step is the last and can sometimes be given short shrift. At this point in the process you may well be tired of looking at the text and think that a superficial review, maybe including a read and spell check, will be sufficient before passing it for review. And you may mistakenly assume someone else, a hired editor, supervisor, whoever, will be happy to clean up your errors. For this book Steve and I have fixed major structural and substantive shortfalls in virtually every one of the twenty plus reviews of the text and Workbook. Still, we constantly fret over what else we might have missed. So from our own experience here is our admonition. Analysts who let someone else fix it do the following:

- **Cede ownership of their work.** Passing on poorly reviewed work invites heavy editing of your hard work and thinking. New errors can be introduced that cascade through the text. There are no easy fixes, and you will be held accountable, not the reviewer.
- **Invite doubts about their analysis.** Reviewers will justifiably conflate poor editing with weak analysis. Consumers, especially if they are new or disagree with the analysis, will use errors discredit it. Trust is lost. And then there are the inevitable phone calls from managers and angry consumers.
- **Risk their reputations.** If analysts are perceived as error prone, peers may resist collaborating then, and managers may well decide to sideline or even replace them.

The point here is that giving this final review short shrift is not just about editing. Do the work.

First Sweep: Message is Clear and Up Front

- Message is evident in the title and lead inference.
- Explains the un-obvious to a generalist.
- Expresses confidence level if appropriate.
- Is consistent throughout the assessment (alignment).
- Is based on data that is credible and cited accurately.
- Answers the decision maker's question.

Second Sweep: Structure Provides Product's "Connective Tissue"

- Each section and paragraph advance the story.
- Text is aligned internally with the B.L.U.F.
- Information related to each theme and topic is grouped together.
- Topic sentences capture a single main point.
- Analytic subtitles tell readers what is ahead.

Third Sweep: Visuals Reinforce Analytic Message

- The analytic point is clear at first glance.
- The message is consistent with the text.
- The visual complements the text (adds detail, explains a point).
- An introductory note ties it to the text.

Fourth Sweep: Error-Free Text Enhances Credibility

- Prose is clear, concise, precise, and expressed in the active voice.
- Grammar is correct.
- Text is free of spelling errors, typos, and dropped text.

EXERCISE: Apply the Four Sweeps to Your Product

Instructions:

Step away from your product for at least a few hours and then work through the review process in Chapter 11 of the Workbook. Be ruthless. Put yourself in the place of your consumer and check carefully through each step. Revise anything that can be misunderstood.

EXERCISE: Refine the B.L.U.F.

Instructions:

Turn to Chapter 11 in the Workbook.

Complete the template using the work you have already done. Don't start over—this happens a lot—you have already done the hard thinking. So, much of this should be simply moving text. The difference, however, is that once completed you will be able to see in one place how the piece holds together. You need to revisit what you have done and make sure you can see the connective tissue that holds it together. If you follow this process you will end up with a clearly outlined B.L.U.F. that can readily be expanded into a longer product.

In addition to the Workbook, we have included another blank template as Appendix B that can be shared for use for future projects.

EPILOGUE

Intelligent Analysis: Tools for the Future

It is a constant in analysts' lives that every word counts every day, and it will remain so. In an increasingly complex and uncertain world inundated with unlimited, often conflicting data, consumers' demand for clearly written, data-driven analysis will only increase and with it so will the value and importance of *Intelligent Analysis*. Regardless of the sources or amount of data, the analysts' tool kit we offer in this book will remain an essential guide to translate that data into actionable intelligence.

Work and Values are Inseparable

This book will serve analysts both practicing or aspiring, now and in the years ahead. Our approach is structured to drive *Intelligent Analysis* regardless of the amount or sources of data. Its step-by-guide is foundational to the work, and the demand for its end product—the B.L.U.F. (yes, that lead paragraph)—will continue to meet a wide range of consumer requirements across private or public sector organizations, academia, and professional schools, as well as in the worlds of science, medicine, law enforcement or civic organizations. More broadly, the book also articulates how you need to approach your work. It is a new way of thinking about yourself in the role of an analyst. The work and the values must always remain inseparable.

As you continue to apply and grow your expertise and analytic skills, we also invite you think about *Intelligent Analysis* as an insurance—or assurance—policy. For the cost of the book and a lot of hard work on your part you acquire a proven set of tools and processes that will make you a more efficient and effective analyst. Our frameworks will help you remain deliberate and conscious about how you shape analytic products and guard against the impact of emotions, biases, and time pressure that will consistently threaten objectivity.

Tailormade for the Era of Artificial Intelligence

The quickly arriving deluge of new information from AI, like Big Data before it, will not change the dynamic relationship between consumers and analysts. Indeed, it will make *Intelligent Analysis* even more central to supporting decision-making and meeting the range of consumer requirements. Regardless of how much data it processes or how quickly or the format of its output, AI will produce only an unvetted answer to your consumer's KIQ. It is still just one data source that is only as good as the assumptions that underpin it. We argue it will still need to be run through the same disciplined process and that it will still come down to producing a well-structured B.L.U.F. Making this point to AI fans who are convinced that AI is the answer should become part of your job.

Risk Culture Matters

Operating across different, sometimes difficult, organizational cultures will also remain a challenge. We expect that analysts and managers in our workshops and courses will continue to lament organizational resistance to new approaches to the work and adherence to rigid formats that just will not work.

We continue to argue that, while organizational culture can be frustrating, *Intelligent Analysis* is its own culture, so a broken organizational culture should not be a barrier. *Intelligent Analysis* is built around being more deliberate and conscious about your work and how you collect and analyze data and express the results in a way that is transparent, defensible, and repeatable. And that standard does not require permission to implement. The organization will only see a better product, and we are confident that other analysts and managers will see that as well. This culture travels well, and because it is about the work and how analysts see themselves, they can carry this standard and spread it throughout their careers regardless of the operating environment. The success it can bring makes *Intelligent Analysis* contagious.

Some last thoughts

- Whether or not you have diligently worked through each step, the central message of *Intelligent Analysis* is "sticky." However lightly, *Intelligent Analysis* is at some level imprinted on your brain's neurons and will surface whenever you write or orally present your analysis. You will have to deliberately ignore its lessons.

- What you say can matter or not. It is your expertise, understanding of the tradecraft and underlying core values that will be your currency as you move through your careers.

- Recognize that you are in a position of high trust, which must be earned and is easily lost.

- You are the eyes and ears of your consumers—a trip wire to warn them of immediate threats or emerging trends that can impact their organizations.
- Trust the process end-to-end and do not skip steps. It is just too dangerous to cut corners.
- Enjoy yourself. Not every day is magical, but just think of the rewards of making a real difference wherever you work and whatever you do.

APPENDIX A

Template: Move the Analytic Product Forward—Build the B.L.U.F.

> **"Writing is thinking. To write well is to think clearly. That's why it's so hard."**
>
> —David McCullough

Complete this template is in the Workbook.

In *Intelligent Analysis* the B.L.U.F. is the deliverable. Remember that when you think you are done, you are not. It can always be better, sharper, more useful to the audience.

Instructions:

Complete this template in the Workbook using the work you have already done. Do not start over—this happens a lot—you have already done the hard thinking. So, much of this should be simply moving text. The difference, however, is that once completed you will be able to see in one place how the piece holds together. You need to revisit what you have done and make sure you can see the connective tissue. If you follow this process you will end up with a clearly outlined B.L.U.F. that can readily be expanded into a longer product. This template can also be printed and/or shared for use in future projects.

Start Below

- What is your working title?
- Who is/are the specific audience(s) for your assessment?
- What is the purpose of your assessment for this/these audience(s)? (inform, warn, target, allocate resources)
- What is your KIQ?
- What data did/will you collect to answer the question?
- How do you plan to array the data?
- List the Working and Key Assumptions that underpin your lead inference.
- What are the Linchpins? (selected after you complete and process the ratings in your KAC)

Now answer the question with the B.L.U.F. Below are the separate B.L.U.F. elements. Use the list of questions below to guide your work, use the follow-on template in the Workbook.

Answer in full sentences. Use your exercises already done in the Workbook to answer these questions—do not start over (happens more than you would think).

- What is the development that made you write?
- Why are you writing now?
- How does it work?
- What has been the impact of the development so far?
- What is the most likely outcome?
- What are the implications of the most likely outcome for your decision maker?
- What mitigation strategies can blunt the risk from your key vulnerabilities?
- Develop indicators of the strategies' effectiveness.

The KAC template is on the next page. It is also in the Workbook.

1. Write out each assumption that underpins the inference: What conditions must persist to maintain the validity of the most likely outcome?	2. How strongly does the data support the inference's estimated probability? (1–10)	3. What is the level of confidence in the data? (1–10)	4. Would this assumption's failure cause any others to fail? (1–10)	5. What is the impact on the inference's estimated probability if the assumption does not hold? (1–10)
One too many				

APPENDIX B

Glossary
Definition of Key Terms

Actionable intelligence: A term used to describe targeted assessments that consumers can act on to meet known requirements; applies to both private and public sector consumers.

Analytic tradecraft: Also known as tradecraft, a term used to describe a set of standardized tools and processes that analysts in the US intelligence services have used for decades to produce consistently objective, data-driven assessments for a wide range of audiences.

Assessment: A conclusion based on underlying intelligence information, analysis, and assumptions.

Assumption: As used in *Intelligent Analysis*, is a condition that must persist to support the estimated level of probability that the consumer will reach the desired outcome, or an event or development will occur; the likelihood must be subject to change with new information. The term "variables" is often used interchangeably but is more closely applicable to economics and math.

Assumptions, working: The first draft of conditions that must persist to support an estimate of probability; can number up to as many as ten or fifteen assumptions.

Assumptions, key: Also called drivers or variables. A list of no more than six assumptions drawn from the list of Working Assumptions considered to be the most important assumptions that must persist to support the estimate of probability. The limit is six because these are the conditions that must persist; dozens of assumptions do not have to persist.

Assumptions, linchpin: The one or two Key Assumptions determined to be the most critical to supporting the estimate of probability; subject to change (more or less certain) with new information. Use of the term in the US intelligence services gained currency in the mid-1990s as a way of focusing analysts' assumptions on what mattered most in assessing the most likely outcome.

Bottom Line on the Bottom (B.L.O.B.): A term that describes a written assessment in which the main point or message does not become apparent until the end of the piece; most common in academic papers and journals but banned in *Intelligent Analysis*.

Bottom Line Up Front (B.L.U.F.): In *Intelligent Analysis* and across the US intelligence services and military, a tightly formatted lead paragraph that provides audiences with actionable intelligence in a complete response to specific audience questions. Each sentence provides a key element of the response, which includes an assessment of the event, the most likely outcome, and why it matters to the consumer.

Caveat: For our purposes, caveats are a group of terms (*likely, unlikely, highly likely, etc....*) used across the US intelligence services to inform or warn consumers of the strength of the relationship between the facts and what can be inferred from those facts. For example, "The event is (likely...) to take place."

Cognitive biases: According to Richards Heuer in *Psychology of Intelligence Analysis*, these are mental errors caused by our simplified information processing strategies: "Cognitive bias does not result from any emotional or intellectual predisposition toward a certain judgment, but rather from subconscious mental processes for interpreting information. A cognitive bias is a mental error that is consistent and predictable."

Consumer: In the context of intelligence analysis, a term used to describe the initiator and end-user of analytic products.

Data-driven analysis: A term used in this book to describe the process of analyzing qualitative or quantitative information to look for trends, patterns, or relationships not readily apparent to decision makers. Transforms data into intelligence. In *Intelligent Analysis*, "data" is the preferred term as opposed to "evidence," which must meet a different standard of certainty.

Debiasing: A term used to describe the reduction of bias, particularly with respect to objective *Intelligent Analysis*.

Estimating the level of probability: Understood as the process of determining the likelihood that a consumer will reach the desired outcome or an event or development will occur, which is described using a set of agreed-upon vocabulary.

Forecast vs. prediction: In this book, the terms are used to distinguish between developing the most likely outcome that is anchored in data (forecast), as opposed to just looking ahead and essentially guessing (prediction).

Indicators: Also known as signposts or indicators of success or change. In *Intelligent Analysis*, they are developed to track the impact of mitigation strategies on the validity of Key Assumptions that support the most likely outcome. They must be observable, based on data, metrics-based, and readily accessible to consumers.

Inference: Defined for our purposes as a conclusion based on facts as known. In this book inferences are structured as A + B → C. A and B are facts as known, and C is the implied inference or insight/conclusion that can be drawn from them. The arrow (→) is a stand-in for the estimate of probability that C will occur (likely, unlikely, etc.) expressed using an agreed-upon vocabulary.

Insider threat: The threat that an employee will use their authorized access, intentionally or unintentionally, to do harm to an organization's mission, resources, reputation, personnel, facilities, information, intellectual property, networks, or systems.

Intelligence: Information inputs of events, non-events, and factors that potentially will shape the most likely outcome.

Intelligence Community Assessment (ICA): The Office of the Director of National Intelligence's premier publication. It is an assessment that is agreed upon by all the US intelligence services.

Intelligence Community Directive (ICD): Standards and policies established by the Director of National Intelligence as the means by which the Office of the Director of National Intelligence provides guidance, policy, and direction to the intelligence community. ICDs that set analytic standards are an example.

Intelligence failure: Defined by the CIA's Center for the Study of Intelligence as a systemic organizational surprise resulting from incorrect, missing, discarded, or inadequate hypotheses.

Internal alignment: In *Intelligent Analysis*, this term is used to describe the consistency of the message throughout an intelligence assessment; that is, the audience sees the same bottom line whether expressed in the title, lead inference, B.L.U.F. section, or the outlook. See probability drift.

Intelligence cycle: Widely used term to describe the steps in the production of *Intelligent Analysis*, which is produced and displayed as a never-ending circle: data requirements collection, processing, analysis, production and dissemination, then back to data requirements again.

***Intelligent Analysis* vs. Intelligence Analysis:** For the purposes of this book, they overlap completely in terms of tools and processes, but use of the term *Intelligent Analysis* is intended to signal utility well beyond their traditional role in the US intelligence services.

Level of confidence (LOC): Defined as a formal assessment of the quality of the data sources measured separately from the level of certainty expressed in the data.

National Insider Threat Task Force: Established as the focal point in the US intelligence community to combat insider threats. NITTF has existed in different iterations since 2002 and has steadily grown in size and mission.

Office of the Director of National Intelligence (ODNI): The Director of National Intelligence serves as the head of the intelligence community, overseeing and directing the implementation of the national intelligence budget and serving as the principal advisor to the president, the National Security Council, and the Homeland Security Council for intelligence matters.

Organizational silence: A term used to describe what occurs in discussions in which participants choose to remain on the sidelines rather than risk criticism or retaliation for speaking out often with serious consequences for the group or, more important the consumer (Morrison and Milliken 2000).

Practical drift: Developed by Scott Snook, who defined it as the slow uncoupling of practice from written procedures (Snook 2000).

Premortem: Included as part of the suite of SATs that, unlike a postmortem, hypothesizes the bad outcome and looks for systemic points of vulnerability.

Probability: Understood here as the likelihood that the desired outcome will be reached or an event or development will occur, expressed in an agreed-upon vocabulary.

Probability drift: *Intelligent Analysis* adopted the term used extensively in probability theory. In intelligence analysis it is the absence of internal alignment; that is, it refers to discrepancies in the estimated level of probability within the same intelligence assessment.

Products: Written components of intelligence analysis such as a B.L.U.F., KIQ, KAC, recommended mitigation strategies, and indicators.

Quantitative data: Understood as information or data based on quantities obtained using a quantifiable measurement process.

Qualitative data: In contrast to quantitative data, this is data that are subjective, including focus groups, interviews, or community meetings.

SAT (SATs): Widely understood as a suite of qualitative frameworks that rely on structured discussions to help analysts mitigate the adverse impact on objective analysis of their cognitive limitations—biases, emotions, and mindsets that work against objective analysis. Their number and utility have expanded over the years, and we use them here to provide templates to use at each step in the *Intelligent Analysis* process.

US intelligence services: The collective term used in this book to describe the US intelligence community, a group of eighteen separate US government intelligence agencies and subordinate organizations that work separately and together to conduct intelligence activities to support foreign policy and national security. The Office of the Director of National Intelligence (ODNI) plays a coordinating role over the US intelligence community and leads the presidential briefing Task Force.

Bibliography

Armstrong, Fulton T. 2007. "Ways to Make Analysis Relevant but Not Prescriptive." Center for the Study of Intelligence.

Cariens, David. 2012. Intelligence and Crime Analysis: Critical Thinking Through Writing. Lake House Publishing.

Center for the Study of Intelligence. 2007. "Words of Estimative Probability." Studies in Intelligence.

Crawford, Kate, "The Hidden Biases of Big Data," Harvard Business Review April 2013

Davenport, Thomas. 2013. "Big Data and the Role of Intuition." Harvard Business Review.

Davis, Jack. 1997. A Compendium of Analytic Tradecraft Notes, vol. 1, notes 1–10. CIA Directorate of Intelligence.

El Nabawi Sherif, Cyber Asia, Defending APAC against malicious insiders and cyber adversaries, July 2020

Federal Bureau of Investigation, The Insider Threat: An Introduction to Detecting and Deterring an Insider Spy (undated)

Fore, Joe. Spring 2020. "Write Like a Spy: Using Intelligence Guidelines to Reinforce Lessons of Predictive Legal Writing." Perspectives: Teaching Legal Southeast Asia, 28, no. 1

Gartin, Joseph. 2019. "The Future of Intelligence," Studies in Intelligence 63(2).

Grusin, Jay and Steve Lindo, Intelligent Analysis: How to Defeat Uncertainty in High-Stakes Decisions, Intelligent Risk Management Publications, 2020 (Amazon)

Grusin, Jay and Steve Lindo. 2018. "Target Canada—A Bad Case of Intelligence Risk Mis-Management." Intelligent Risk Management LLC.

Heuer, Richards J., Jr. 1999. Psychology of Intelligence Analysis. Center for the Study of Intelligence, Central Intelligence Agency.

Intelligence Community Assessment, Global Water Security, ICA 2012-08, February 2012

Intelligence Community Directives (ICD) 203

Klein, G. (2007). "Performing a Project Premortem". Harvard Business Review. 85 (9): 18–19.

Major, James S. 2009. Communicating with Intelligence. Professional Intelligence Series, no 1. Concept Publishing.

McCollugh, David, Writing is thinking. "To write well is to think clearly. That's why it's so hard."

(Interview with NEH chairman Bruce Cole, Humanities, July/Aug. 2002, Vol. 23/ No. 4)

Morrison, Elizabeth Wolfe, and Francis J. Milliken. 2000. "Organizational Silence: A Barrier to Change and Development in a Pluralistic World." Academy of Management Review 25(4).

National Intelligence Council. 2012. Global Water Security. Intelligence Community Assessment.

National Intelligence Estimate (NIE). 2002. Iraq's Continuing Programs for Weapons of Mass Destruction. (Declassified Key Judgments.)

Office of the Director of National Intelligence. 2006. Intelligence Community Directive 201: National Foreign Intelligence Warning System.

Office of the Director of National Intelligence. 2015. Intelligence Community Directive 203: Analytic Standards.

Office of the Director of National Intelligence. 2016. Intelligence Community Directive 206: Sourcing Requirements for Disseminated Analytic Products.

Orwell, George, "Why I Write," 1946

Petersen, Martin. 2011. "What I learned in 40 Years of Doing Intelligence Analysis for US Foreign Policymakers." Studies in Intelligence 55(1).

Pfeffer, Jeffrey and Robert Sutton. 2006. "Evidence-Based Management." Harvard Business Review.

Ramsey, Diane M. and Mark S. Boerner. 1995. "A Study in Indications Methodology." Center for the Studies of Intelligence.

Silver, Nate, 2012, The Signal and the Noise, Why Some Predictions Fail—But Some Don't, The Penguin Press, 2012.

Sinclair, Robert. 2010. "Thinking and Writing: Cognitive Science and Intelligence Analysis." Center for the Study of Intelligence. (Originally published in January 1984.)

Snook, Scott, 2000. Friendly Fire: The Accidental Shootdown of U.S. Black Hawks over Northern Iraq

Taleb, Nassim, 2010, The Black Swan, Random House.

Taleb, Nassim, 2001, Fooled By Randomness, Texere.

Taleb, Nassim N. 2008a. Interview with Constantine Sandis. Philosophy Now.

Taleb, Nassim N. 2008b. "The Fourth Quadrant: A Map of The Limits of Statistics." The Edge, September 15.

Talend Solutions, What is Data Reliability? Undated

US Government. 2009. A Tradecraft Primer: Structured Analytic Techniques for Improving Intelligence Analysis.

US Intelligence Services. "Quality Framework." This is a composite from several examples.

Walton, Tim. Consumer Knowledge, Collaboration Shape Key Intelligence Question, undated.

Walton, Tim. Intelligence Question Framework "Embodying Standards: in a Textbook, Sherman Kent School for Intelligence Analysis at CIA." Presentation undated

Wilder, Dennis, An Educated Consumer is Our Best Customer, Studies in Intelligence Vol. 55, No. 2 (Extracts, June 2011).

Zinsser, William, On Writing Well (6th ed) , 1998.

Made in the USA
Monee, IL
04 November 2026

67387157R00108